RAPID VIZ

A New Method for the Rapid
Visualization of Ideas

Hanks and Belliston

CRISP.
Learning

Menlo Park, California

© 1990 by Crisp Publications, Inc.
Printed in the United States of America
by Von Hoffmann Graphics, Inc.

CrispLearning.com

00   01   02   13   12   11   10   9

ISBN 1-56052-055-8 Paper Edition

Hanks, Kurt, 1947-
    Rapid viz: a new method for the rapid
visualization of ideas / Hanks and Belliston
       p. cm.
    Reprint.   Originally published:
    Experimental ed. Los Altos, Calif.
: W. Kaufmann, c1980.
    Includes bibliographical references.
    ISBN 1-56052-055-8 : $15.95
    1. Graphic arts—Technique. 2. Felt marker
drawing. 3. Visual communication. 4. Drawing,
Psychology of. I. Belliston, Larry, 1949-   .
II. Title.
[NC877.8.H36 1990]
741.6—dc20   90-21967
                                 CIP

This book was designed by:
Information
Design
3357 South 2300 East
Salt Lake City, Utah 84109

Sources for the illustrations accompanied by small numbers are listed in the Credits.

Contents

... the learning to visualize of two inseparable images, one on a sheet of paper and the other on the back of your mind.

"All we need is ~~WANT~~ another drawing book."

When I mentioned to an architect friend of mine that I was thinking of writing a book on drawing he just stared at me. Then he bellowed with hands waving in the air, "All we need is another drawing book. Why you could fill this room with those kinds of books. There are thousands of them covering everything you could possibly want to know about drawing." He pointedly asked, "Why on earth would you want to do another?"

It is a good question. Why would I want to do another? The answer comes from personal experience. It involves my own development; I ~~what~~ want to explain to you what I feel drawing, thinking, visualizing is all about.

My visual education began later in life than it does for most people. It began when I was in college. My only previous exposure was doodling on scraps of paper around the borders of English themes and on the pages of the phone book and such random places. In college I floated around various majors but finally landed in design. In that college you had to learn to draw if you wanted to get your ideas across. Drawing was something you were made to learn—something you had to go through and get over with like chicken pox.

And so I did it; after taking several classes, considerable effort, and filling waste baskets with discarded drawings, I finally reached an acceptable level of proficiency. But the whole education process seemed too long and too involved; too filled with unnecessary and inefficient teaching for what I finally gained.

I realized, however, that something else had happened along the way. Yes, I had learned to draw; but more importantly, I learned to *think*. My whole method of thinking experienced a complete switch. I began to *see* the world more clearly. As my hand sketched the lines, my mind revealed a whole new method of thinking that I had not known before. Being able to visualize things gave me a tool that I could use in all facets of life. What happened to my mind was much more important than the sketches I produced.

This is the kind of drawing we are talking about, not the other one.

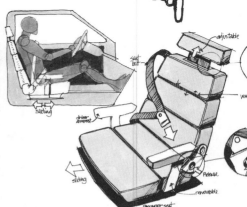

1

Learning to use pen and paper had thus revealed talents I didn't know I had. Not the great talents of a fine *artist* that you might expect, but the important, practical ability to visualize. I gained the ability to picture something mentally, then quickly convert those thoughts into visual reality on a piece of paper. I could nail my ideas down on a sheet of paper.

I realized that converting these ideas had to be a rapid process taking a minimum amount of time, trouble, and work. An idea is a very delicate or fleeting thing and if it is not quickly crystalized into reality it just slips away never to be found again. A rapid conversion from thought to paper is critical.

I found myself asking the question, "Can this new-found skill be taught to others?" "And can it be done without all the hassle, redundancy, and expense I had gone through in my own education?" As so often happens in life, I found myself eating all those bad words I said about teachers: I became a teacher. In a classroom situation I began to challenge students to learn the kind of drawing that had become such a valuable asset in my life.

For the next couple of years, we (it was always a group effort) evolved a method that worked. The students helped me reduce drawing to the essentials. We developed not a *fine art* type of drawing, but a simplified approach that people can use for thinking, learning, and communicating.

This book is an outgrowth of classroom teaching. By trial and error we discovered the best teaching approach. I hope that you, too, will gain by the experience many students went through to develop this condensed teaching approach.

About This Book

Some of the objectives and guidelines used to develop this book were to:

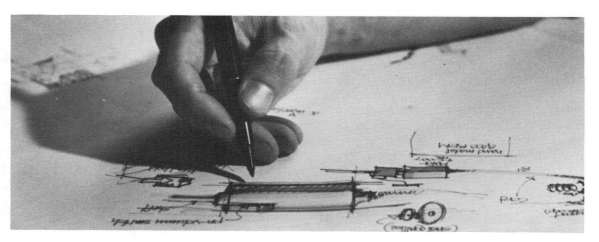

1. Produce a practical workbook to help individuals visualize their thoughts.

2. Use examples and exercises that have been tried by students.

3. Use tools, technology and definitions that relate to a student's understanding.

4. Design the content of the book for people and students in architecture, landscape architecture, engineering, industrial design, interior design, and for students and other practitioners of many basic sciences and arts in which visualization is vital.

5. Emphasize speed in mastering actions and concepts, reducing time, effort, and cost of learning.

6. Use materials and equipment that are easily attainable and economical.

7. Structure the information from simple to complex, from concrete to abstract, from general to specific.

8. Apply visualization to real-life situations whenever possible.

9. Have students learn by doing. (Although visualization is more a mental process than a physical one, the mental process is learned by actually doing.)

10. Provide positive reinforcement to the student to prove that he *can* draw and visualize his own ideas.

Earlier Education Sometimes Hampers Our Thinking

Through my teaching, I found that often the less you know about drawing the better off you will be in learning to visualize. The less you know, the fewer the preconceived ideas you have about drawing and visualizing. You don't have to unlearn things. I can remember one class in particular where I had two separate groups. One group was made up of architecture and landscape architecture students who had had what amounted to a lot of previous drawing experience. The other group was made up of beginning interior design students who had no experience—they had no idea even what a "T square" was. At first the experienced group excelled over the inexperienced group. But the interior design students who had no drawing experience just kept plodding along until, in the end, their performance exceeded the more experienced students' performance. Experience often breeds arrogance and indifference to what may seem simplistic and rudimentary exercises. But simplicity has an uncanny way of positioning itself behind genious.

Getting the Most Out of This Book

Please do more than just read this book. If you only read and do no more, it won't work. The book must be used to be of any value to you. Write in it, draw in it, insert your own pages in it, and do whatever else seems helpful to you.

Far too often education becomes too restrictive, filled with constraints and negative comments. The only possible result is to make the student an outsider—a bystander looking in. But to really understand anything you must actually do it. Second-hand learning from someone else telling you about it never is very effective.

You can't learn to visualize by osmosis. Over the years, I've had a lot of students who have tried. They seem afraid to fail; scared of criticism about their awkward sketches. But they—and you—should not be. Learning anything takes time, involves making mistakes, and involves effort. No one has learned to walk without walking—no one has learned to visualize without drawing.

I hear and I forget.
I see and I remember.
I do and I understand.

4   (An old Chinese saying)

The Drawing Cycle

The Brain

The Eye

The Hand

The Image

The brain is like a muscle that must be used. If not used, it atrophies and becomes weak and ineffective. With Rapid Visualization the brain *muscle* is connected to other muscles in the hand. Coupled with the eye, the brain and muscles make a continuous cycle of expression and feedback that enables you to transfer thoughts from your head to expressions on paper where they can be refined and recorded.

What I really want to encourage is participation. Between you and me through this book and a participation between your mind, your hand, and your eyes. All this participation is important. As we noted earlier about visualization, drawing is more a mental process than a physical one, but it is learned by physically doing. You have to push those thoughts out of your mind with a pencil, then draw and develop them before your eyes on paper.

Make this book yours. Force it to give you what you need. Don't separate yourself from your own education. By itself this book is not the best method for learning—not as good as a classroom situation—so you must force the book to fill your needs. You must take an active part in your own learning process.

(By the way, my architect friend who expressed so much skepticism about this book eventually changed his mind. He helped refine and develop the book. There is a great need for rapid visualization in his profession and many others also.)

"I do not think that we have begun to scratch the surface of training in visualization."

Jerome S. Bruner
Educational Psychologist

There are at least two ways of learning and knowing something. One way is the usual way taught in the educational system—the 3 r's of reading, writing, and arithmetic. With this method you read something, you memorize it, and you are supposed to be able to recall what you learned.

There are also other ways to learn and know something. One way involves the "I feel" method. You know something because you *feel* it.

Drawing is more the feeling or intuitive kind of learning and knowing than it is the sequential, rote memorization kind of learning. Drawing leans very much toward the holistic or intuitive side of the brain.

An example of "feeling" learning is when I learned to shoot a rifle at targets thrown into the air. As a youngster I took pride in my ability to shoot accurately. One day a friend and I went shooting together—he outclassed me terribly. He was a magnificent shot. And I wanted to be at least as good a shot as he was.

I had heard about a method of shooting wherein you shot from the hip without taking aim. You aimed by "feel" rather than by looking down the sights of the gun. So I set out to learn this "feeling" method of shooting.

Another person would throw items into the air and I would shoot from the hip. It's like pointing your finger—you don't need to look down your finger to know that you are pointing in the right direction. As I became able to hit the thrown targets, I progressed to shooting them from a greater distance. Then I progressed to smaller and smaller targets until I became very proficient at shooting moving targets in the air.

I became a very good shot eventually by "feel." You may assume that the best way to learn to shoot is by looking down the sights of a gun.

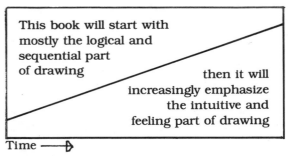

This book will start with mostly the logical and sequential part of drawing then it will increasingly emphasize the intuitive and feeling part of drawing

Time ——▷

But know that I became a better shot by "feeling" than by the logical, traditional method. And my friend even improved his magnificent shooting ability by adopting the "feeling" method I had learned.

Intuition vs. Logic

Another example of relying on "feelings" or "intuition" is speed reading. Conventional reading experts will tell you that it's impossible to read a book in 10 minutes and comprehend what you read. But some speed readers do it all the time and have better comprehension than regular slower readers have.

What's their secret? They "feel" what they read. They give you correct answers because they "feel" the answers are right. They don't rely on logic and sequence to recall what they read. Speed readers utilize the visual, intuitive, holistic half of the brain.

Visualization is to drawing as shooting by feeling is to shooting by the sight method. Visualization is to drawing as speed reading is to conventional reading.

Let me describe how it works in drawing. You know what perspective drawing is—that's where you draw things in three dimensions, giving the appearance of distance and volume. The conventional method is a laborious method of connecting lines and projecting images. It is an elaborate method of drawing that is difficult to understand, more difficult to

5

Principles don't load us down with too much hardware.

Principles don't leave us bare without sufficient protection.

Principles provide sufficient tools for our journey.

learn, and very difficult to do well. It's no wonder many artists don't do perspective well.

A teacher once told me there is no other way to do perspective than by the conventional method. Wrong! The rapid visualization method is better and easier. To prove it, I have taken students that seemed to have equal abilities. To one student I taught the usual elaborate perspective method. To the other student I taught the rapid visualization method.

Invariably, the rapid visualization method works better. The "rapid viz" student learns in a few minutes rather than a few hours. And the end result is unquestionably better than the work done by the student who uses the conventional method.

Rapid Visualization

I've found it easier to teach rapid visualization by starting in a logical sequential manner—the

conventional teaching method. If a radical new concept like rapid viz is taught in a radical new way people feel overwhelmed. So I teach the new rapid viz concept in a traditional way at first. Through a slow transition in this book you'll switch from the logical and sequential to intuitive learning. The book proceeds first from logical, very understandable, and simplified ways of drawing to the intuitive methods later on (possibly without your knowing it).

I've consistently done two things throughout this book. First, the information is presented as "principles." Second, exercises push you to the limit of your abilities.

Why principles? By teaching basic principles you will be able to apply rapid viz to many situations. It's like teaching a man to fish to satisfy his hunger rather than giving the man a fish to eat. Principles, though short and concise, are much more filling—much richer.

Also, principles allow you to travel light and fast. And that's important. You need the knowledge necessary to make quick decisions. You won't be drawing masterpieces for the National Gallery of Art. You'll be doing quick sketches that expand and refine your thoughts.

The second thing I said I'd do is push you to the limit of your abilities. It's important that you be pushed. In speed reading you don't become a speed reader unless you push to read faster than is comfortable. Likewise push yourself to draw faster than is comfortable. You need to force yourself to do the exercises at ever increasing speed.

You've heard the saying "work expands to fill the time alloted." I've had students take 2 hours if given 2 hours, 3 days if given 3 days, or 5 minutes if given 5 minutes. You will be pleasantly surprised to find yourself doing things you didn't believe possible.

But it won't be without effort or without error. You're going to make mistakes. That's part of the program. You learn from mistakes as well as from successes. You must try to push beyond your limits. I'm going to give you exercises to do that are impossible to do within the time alloted. You will learn and grow from trying, not from completing the exercise.

Play

Play. That's another important part of pushing yourself. This is all one big game to have fun at. And when you win, the rewards will be better than you may imagine.

Little children gain confidence in their ability to cope with life by role playing. "Let's play house; you be the father, I'll be the mother, and little Susie will be the baby." You need to play with rapid viz to gain confidence.

If you take things too seriously it will be self defeating. Don't worry about how well you're doing, just do it.

Don't look at your drawings and get discouraged. Don't meticulously try to fix things. If you're like most people you will get discouraged and question your own ability. Don't. Remember, have fun at it!

Drawing is important to mind expansion. You can't really develop that other half of your mind without some activity like drawing to get things going. But you should feel open and confident and that comes from play. Nobody should laugh at your first funny, crummy, lousy little drawings more than you do. Don't be afraid to goof-up.

To sum it up—principles will help you travel light and travel quick; and in order to grow you will need to be pushed beyond your abilities so go do it! Have fun and don't worry about your failings.

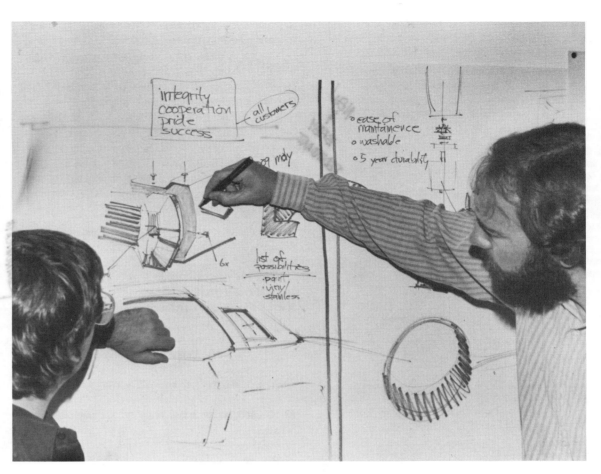

Fear of failure, fear of criticism are among the reasons people don't learn to visualize.

The Bilingual Mind

Let's talk for a moment about words. It's tough to imagine living without them, isn't it? Is it possible? A baby gets along for a time without words. He tells his mother when he's hungry—or tired, insecure, in pain, wet? But the baby's communication is hit and miss without language—mother may check the new baby's diaper when it is really gas pains that cause him to cry. We would live a fairly isolated existence without words. Words then are tools that help us communicate to others our needs, our feelings, and our thoughts. They facilitate interaction between individuals.

[handwritten note: NEW & BABY REDUNDANT]

Language also helps us express our feelings. Wouldn't it be frustrating to be in love and not let others know? Or to feel anger and not be able to vocalize it? Give something a name, a word, and it makes sense. In trying to tell the doctor about an unusual pain, you may use phrases such as "It felt like . . .," "It was between here and here, but it wasn't really . . .," "I thought it was this, only it was similar

[handwritten note: COMMUNICATE]

to . . .," and so on. Then the doctor diagnoses it—labels it—and it becomes something real. Can something exist without words to identify it?

A View of Reality

Language gives us a viewpoint on reality and enables us to formulate thoughts. Think of a concept and try to disassociate it from words. It's hard to give an example because examples necessitate using words. Picture yourself swimming (don't think of the words pool and water), or eating (without the words food, fork, plate, etc.). Words help us organize and structure our thoughts.

Knowledge and language are inseparable. The transfer of knowledge is limited by our ability to conceptualize and *symbolize* thoughts. This requires some kind of language. What good is a great idea or thought if it can never leave the abyss of the mind? What if every person who wanted to fly had to start from scratch because

Two separate points of view

One language and way of thinking
Visual
Intuitive
Holistic

Another language and way of thinking
Sequential
Verbal
Logical

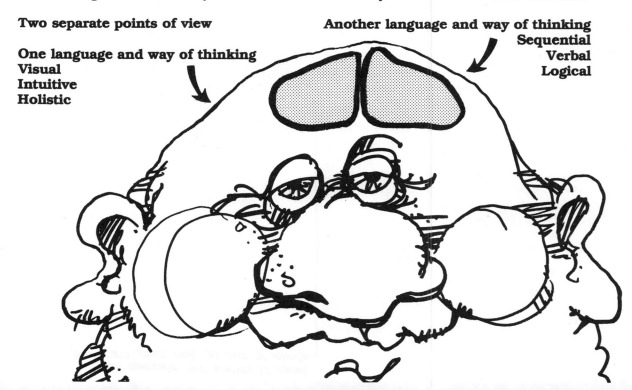

no language existed to convey the experience of flying to others? Aviation would never have progressed to the Wright brothers' prototype—or beyond.

So language is vital. But, if one language is good, aren't two languages better? A second language enables us to better express ourselves. A few examples: we call that white stuff which precipitates from the heavens in the winter *snow*. Sometimes it's so heavy and wet that just shoveling a path to the front door requires a herculean effort. Sometimes it's so light and fluffy that you can't resist the urge to romp and play. Here are two quite different substances—only one name, snow. But the Eskimos' language has about fifty different terms for what we call snow. Similarly, the Arabs have dozens of words for plain old sand. If we knew a second language, we might not be handicapped by a limited set of words.

ONLY IF YOU SPOKE TO SOMEONE ELSE WHO UNDERSTOOD THAT LANGUAGE

A Second Language

A second language also might increase our perceptions of the world around us. If you visit a foreign city where you do not know the language, how much of that city can you actually perceive without being able to read the billboards, the shop names, the window signs? If you were in Spain, for example, you might be able to identify a factory by its exterior, but without knowing Spanish, the sign Muebles hanging on the outside wouldn't clue you in to the fact that they are manufacturing furniture inside. A second language expands our perceptions, thus increasing our experience and our knowledge.

When we speak of a second language, French, German, Spanish, or some other foreign tongue automatically comes to mind. In this book we're going to learn another language, a second language, but one that has no nouns.

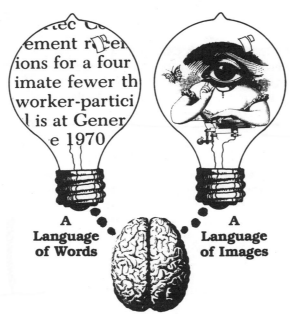

A
Language of Words

A
Language of Images

verbs, adjectives or adverbs. Like a foreign language, it will enable you to better express yourself and to increase your perceptions of the world around you. It's a language of the mind.

Two Minds in One

Our mind is a fascinating instrument. The brain actually has two distinct and separate halves. The left half controls the right side of your body, and vice versa. Each half of your brain also controls different skills and abilities. The left hemisphere is probably your analytical half. It is concerned with order, logic, and reason. It controls your verbal and written skills. The right hemisphere is primarily responsible for your visual thinking. It enables you to recognize faces and objects. Intuition, fantasy, creativity are controlled by this half of the brain. A typical education develops primarily the analytical skills—reading, writing, and arithmetic—the left half. The visual-thinking hemisphere assumes a subordinate role and is seldom if ever developed to its full potential.

A second language, the language of the brain, is initially taught in preschool and kindergarten years. Parents and teachers are continually giving children crayons and paper—not with the goal of teaching them visual expression, unfortunately, but to keep them out of mischief. Painting and drawing are considered by many to be frivolous activities, and the educational process soon replaces them with more scientific, literary learning. The visual language is underutilized, neglected, and eventually lost.

But which language, verbal or visual, is actually the basic or primary language of the mind? Early man didn't leave behind cave dwellings adorned with vocabulary words and mathematical formulas. He used pictures to communicate how he lived. Before children are taught the verbal tools for self-expression they intrinsically know how to use scissors, crayons and paper to reflect their perceptions of the world.

Develop Another Language— A Visual Language

The purpose of this book is to help you learn that second language of visual expression. Does the world really need it? Here are some examples. You decide.

Example 1

An airline serves five northeastern cities within a twelve-hour period—Concord, New Hampshire; Albany, New York; Danbury, Connecticut; Elmira, New York; and Boston, Massachusetts. Their flights run from Boston to Concord, Danbury to Concord, Albany to Boston, Concord to Elmira, Albany to Elmira, Concord to Danbury, Boston to Albany, Concord to Albany. What is the shortest way to make a round trip from Albany to Danbury?

HOPEFULLY, MOST PARENTS DO GIVE CRAYONS TO CHILDREN FOR THE PURPOSES OF CREATIVITY, CHALENGE AND EXPRESSION. PARENTS THAT GIVE CRAYONS TO CHILDREN TO KEEP THEM FROM MISCHIEF ARE LAZY!!

QUITE A LOT IF YOU JUST OBSERVE WHAT IS GOING ON AROUND YOU.

A verbal approach would require establishing some arbitrary set of order. Let's try the typical one, alphabetical:

- Albany to Boston
- Albany to Elmira
- Boston to Albany
- Boston to Concord
- Concord to Albany
- Concord to Danbury
- Concord to Elmira
- Danbury to Concord

The solution is still not readily apparent. Now try a diagrammatic approach:

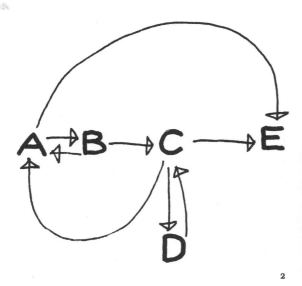

Or better yet:

Example 2

A football play is another example of communicating with different means. You can verbally describe a particular play from scrimmage. You can explain with photographs. Or you can use visual diagrams (rapid viz) to communicate the message.

An example of explaining the football play in verbal terms would read something like this.

When the ball is hiked, the four interior linemen step back about 2-3 steps to assume pass protection blocking. The two backfield men cross in the middle to assume blocking position for quarterback pass protection. The right end is to run a down and out pass pattern making the cut to the outside about ten yards beyond the line of scrimmage. The left end . . . It's obvious from the example that a verbal explanation is hard to understand.

A photographic explanation is also somewhat difficult to understand. One photo, as shown, looks like a mass of confusion. It would take an aerial shot of many photos in sequence to explain what is happening.

2

3

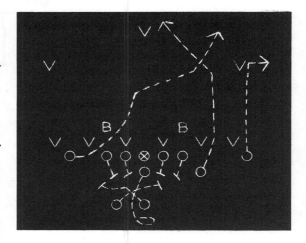

A rapid viz type diagram is the most economical way to communicate this particular play. The single, simple diagram shown clearly communicates what the plan is.

Example 3
Can you imagine the complexity of house plans if they were expressed in the verbal language? A one-page drawing would become a multi-paged document.

Summary

Which doctor would you rather have operate on you? A doctor who had memorized the parts of the body from strictly a verbal text and could only verbally describe a muscle or a bone from what he had read, or a doctor who had actually seen the ventricles of the heart and who had a vital working knowledge of the body.

Regardless of your profession, age, intellect, or motor skills, you can learn to speak that second language—the language of the mind. Without it you'll forever be using only half of your mental capacity. With it you'll know two ways of thinking, communicating, learning, being. So let's begin now to expand your visual mind.

What you need to get started

A frightening thing awaits you. It has made strong men cry and sent women fleeing from its very presence. It is a blank piece of paper. What are you going to do with it? What threat lies beyond its snowy white innocence? You are going to have to make a mark on it—you are about to violate its purity. Can you do it? Of course you can.

First you will need materials. You can play the game that some illustrators/designers play, which is to buy the "very best" special made guaranteed for 40 years or 40,000 miles writing pen; or you can buy a simple felt tip pen. I recommend the simple pen that's cheap, easy to use, and always there when you need it. For now get any pen or pencil you can find. We'll have none of this "I can't go on with the work because my special order pen has not arrived from Walla Walla."

Use whatever you want as long as it's simple, cheap, and you can carry it in your pocket or purse at all times. Don't be one of those designers who is crippled without special drawing tools.

The kind of pen I prefer is a simple felt tip pen with a flexible point. Flair, EG, and Pentel (to name a few) make the inexpensive pens that I like. The only really important thing to me is that the point be able to draw thick lines when I press down firmly or thin lines when I use a light touch. Ball point pens don't allow this flexibility.

You may decide upon a pencil. I like drawing with pencils but prefer that *you* begin with a pen. With a pencil you can easily erase and *fix up* rapid drawings. You should be learning to do rapid drawings correctly the first time, not learning to *fix up* drawings. A pencil causes many people to become "fix up" artists. You need to be committed—once the pen makes a mark the deed is done. So, for now, use a pen; save the pencil for later.

When it comes time for the pencil, what pencil should you buy? Pencils are rated 6H (hard) to 6B (soft). If you like to scratch your message in the surface with a nail, then 6H is your pencil. If you are a real soft touch, then 6B is the one for you. For me, 2H feels right—not too hard, not too soft.

And Everyone Makes Mistakes

Also, you may want an eraser, in spite of my earlier remarks about erasing. To erase pen lines drawn with a felt tip pen, I wet the end of a pencil eraser. To erase pencil lines I use a kneaded eraser.

You may want to keep a ruler handy as well as a variety of colors of felt tip pens. I find it fun to draw in black then use some other color to add emphasis. The second color is my way of doodling with a drawing. You won't need other colors or a straight edge, but then again you may find them fun.

Many people have the tendency to load themselves down with tools they cannot afford, cannot easily use, and don't really need.

11

Going back to that blank sheet referred to earlier, you will need paper to write on. First of all, use the paper in this book. If I request an exercise be done in the book, do it! Don't be afraid of ruining the book; it is a workbook. It's not a book to look pretty on your library shelf. If you do not intend to do the exercises in the book, it is best not to buy it.

You'll need two other kinds of drawing paper. A good basic paper is regular bond paper, the kind you write and type on. Most drawings will be done on cheap bond paper.

You'll also need tracing paper. In one part of the book we cover how to evolve drawings. To evolve a drawing you will need to trace and refine your initial sketches. I prefer a 14" x 17" pad of tracing paper that is easy to see through but strong enough not to tear when you write on it. The least expensive paper you can buy that will do those things is the kind you should buy.

The ultimate goal is to have the tools fuse with yourself.

You need to get to know your pen so that it becomes an extension of your hand. Your pen becomes part of you. You need to become so familiar with it that you don't think about it. This comes from drawing or doodling a lot.

A tennis player's racket becomes an extension of the player's arm and hand. He automatically knows how far it will reach to hit the ball. Until a tennis player becomes familiar with the racket, he can't play tennis well. And the way a player learns to control that racket is to hit tennis balls. He doesn't jump right in and plan a championship game first time out. He just hits the ball around—at walls, fences, other players, or over the fence.

You are like the beginning tennis player. You are trying to fuse your hand permanently to the pen. The way you do this is by drawing. Scribble or doodle often. Practice every chance you get.

A Critical Drawing Tool—The Line

Lines are the first drawing technique you will learn. And there's good reason for learning lines:

1. Line drawing is a quick way to visualize ideas with a minimum use of time and materials.
2. Line drawing tools and materials are usually the easiest to use and least expensive.
3. Line drawing is the natural way to draw—children begin with line and adults usually continue with it as they doodle throughout life.
4. Line emphasizes the basic structure and composition of a drawing which ensures more probable success and a more effective sketch.
5. Line provides a framework on which to hang other drawing techniques such as shading and color.

6. Line is easy to reproduce on copy and blueprint machines.

Now you have the necessary tools. You are ready. It's time to begin. The next page has the first exercise.

The first few exercises are really easy. Maybe even a little too easy. The important thing is for you to begin to do *something*. Get familiar with your pen and paper.

Start with lines. Make some lines with your pen—thick lines and thin lines. Try different pressures on the pen point. Lay the pen down on the paper; use the side of the pen tip to draw a line.

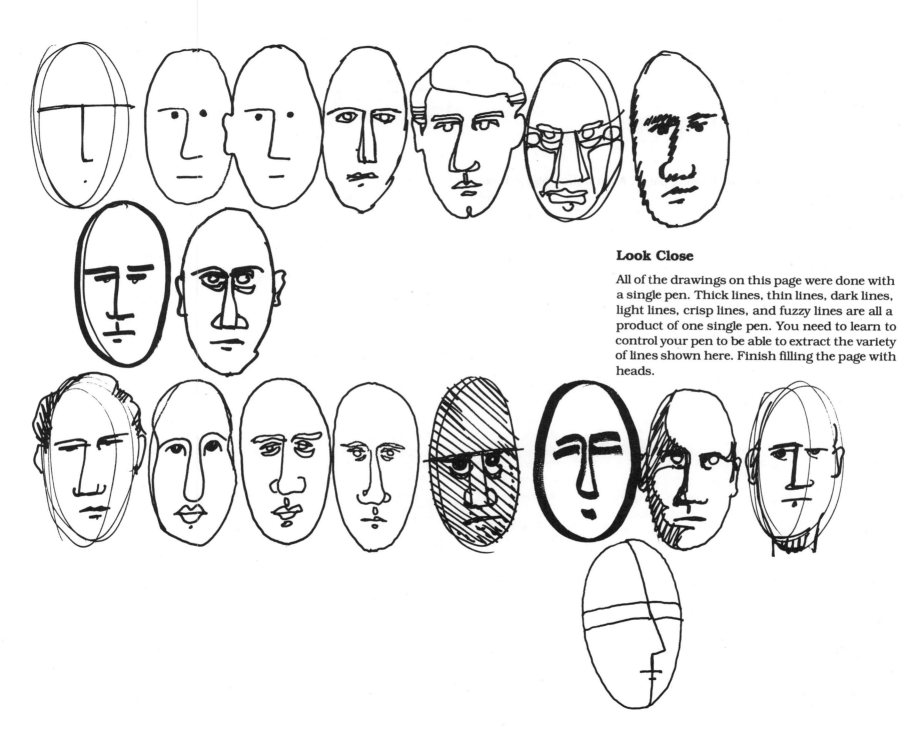

Look Close

All of the drawings on this page were done with a single pen. Thick lines, thin lines, dark lines, light lines, crisp lines, and fuzzy lines are all a product of one single pen. You need to learn to control your pen to be able to extract the variety of lines shown here. Finish filling the page with heads.

13

Visual Thinking

Like any kind of thinking, visual thinking becomes easier and more productive the more you do it. The mind has been compared to a muscle in that it performs better the more it is used.

Visual Thinking Games

In an attempt to get your mind in the groove of thinking visually, try the following visual games. First, draw any doodle. Ask a partner to make something from the doodle. Here's an example of how it's done.

☐ *Now you make something from your doodles. Quality of drawing is not an important consideration. The exercise is to teach visual thinking. Just be sure that your drawings are recognizable.*

☑ *Check the box as you complete each exercise.*

What Is It?

Another fun game is to try to guess what the objects are when an incomplete view is shown. Your mind is forced to imagine what the drawing would be if seen from a more complete view or if the rest of the drawing were visible.

14

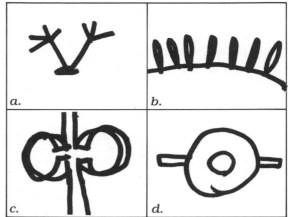

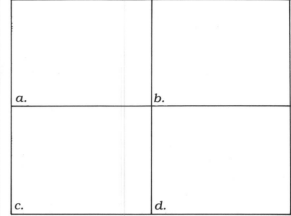

☐ *Look at the squares above. I'll tell you what the drawings represent so that you get the feel of how the exercise works.*
a. *early bird getting the worm*
b. *just before Custer's last stand*
c. *a flamingo swallowing a barbell*
d. *a Mexican wearing a sombrero riding a bicycle*

☐ *Below are some other drawings. You imagine what you think the drawings represent. The answers are shown on the next page.*

☐ *Using incomplete pictures as in the previous examples, you draw the following things in the squares above:*
a. *a porcupine's pillow*
b. *Abraham Lincoln taking a bath*
c. *a spider doing a handstand*
d. *the other side of the argument*

☐ *In the last two sets of squares make up your own visuals. (If you are tempted not to do this exercise, reconsider. Learning to think in visual patterns is accomplished by practicing. It is an easy, fun exercise, so try it.)*
a. _____
b. _____
c. _____
d. _____

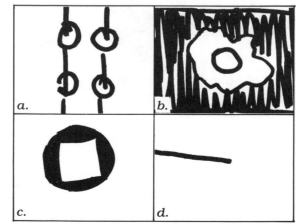

4

Getting the Picture

Most all of us have, at one time or another, played the game of guessing what we see in cloud formations. The puffy clouds indicate images to our mind. This next visual game is very similar to that.

☐ *Shown are a bunch of squiggly lines. A series of sentences describe the lines. You match the sentence with the squiggle. Note: in some instances it isn't necessary that you see a distinct image in the lines, you might just get a certain "feel" that says to your visual mind what the sentence says.*

a.   b.   c.   d.   e.

—He had learned the amazing ability from his brother's dog.

—After laboring for weeks she was ready for the unveiling.

—The wierd Gopile stomped down main street consuming everything in its path.

—How long it had been there was impossible to determine.

—61-year-old Maude hadn't ever been married; indeed, it was doubtful she ever had a suitor.

☐ *Make up your own squiggles and sentences to describe what they mean. Remember, there is no single right answer. It is an intuitive exercise.*

Key Principles

A number of key statements will help you understand what this book intends to accomplish. Some of the exercises may seem strange, but every exercise has been calculated and tested to be effective in accomplishing a specific purpose. Listed are the goals for the book and the methods that it uses to reach them.

1. The intent of the book is to help you develop your own unique style of visual expression. It is not trying to help you become a master illustrator, just a visual thinker. The exercises take you from copying someone else's visuals to making your own. As the book progresses, you should develop a style that is comfortable for you.

2. You must push yourself. Becoming better at drawing is similar to other skills in that you must push beyond current capabilities in order to improve. A weight lifter improves by trying to lift heavier pieces. A runner improves by running faster or for longer periods of time. Push your abilities—strive for better work in shorter periods of time.

3. Defer judgment. One of the biggest pitfalls to learning visual skills is the tendency to judge. "My drawings look silly compared to those in the book," you might say. That's judging. Don't judge. Just do the exercises.

4. Humor helps defer judgment. Many artists criticize the cartoons and nonsense drawings in a book like this. The purpose of the humor is to get the student to laugh. If you can laugh at your drawings, it's easier to defer judgment. Taking things too seriously too early in the learning process discourages some would-be visual thinkers.

5. Set tight parameters. The exercises attempt to restrict your freedom at least for now. Tight restrictions as to what is to be drawn, how long to take, and so forth make drawing easier at first. Do the same for yourself. Set tight goals. Too many choices breed confusion and non-performance. Decide specifically what to do and then do it.

6. Rapid viz is a progressive process. You will learn a little at a time. Go back over things to determine your own improvement. Progress in small steps rather than trying to become proficient in one big step.

7. Learn in sequence. Some things are more easily learned after first learning preparatory skills. Such is the case with many of the rapid viz techniques. Take things in order as much as possible.

8. As you proceed through the book you will be asked to draw things that may not interest you. "Why draw interiors of buildings if I am a landscape architect?" you may ask yourself. The answer is that the techniques you learn are the same no matter what you draw. What you learn by drawing objects different from your area of work or study will be beneficial to you.

9. Keep records of your progress. Check each exercise. Save the drawings that you do. Record the date or sequence you did things in. As you look back over previous work you will be surprised to note the progress.

10. This book is not the ideal teaching medium. A live teacher would be better, but this is a good alternative. The techniques have been tested with live students. Although learning will take effort on your part, the effort expended will be worth the rewards. Learning rapid viz will not only change your drawing habits, it will expand your thinking abilities.

---

a. *a bear climbing a telephone pole*
b. *the view of the sun through a chuck hole*
c. *a square peg in a round hole*
d. *the end of the line*

The Box
Method

One of the most difficult things for people to learn is to draw in correct perspective. Teachers have struggled for years to find methods to teach students to draw correct perspective rapidly and quickly. I have found a method that works well. It is easy to learn. It will work every time. And, even if you have no art background whatever, using this method you will be able to draw accurate perspective.

The method involves a box or cube. If you can draw a two-dimensional square correctly, you then can easily draw a box. If you can draw a box in accurate perspective, you can draw anything, accurately and in perspective.

Sounds simple, doesn't it? It is simple. It will take some practice. It will take time to understand what is happening. You will have to practice those things mentioned in this book. But, if you do, you will find it is really quite easy.

Cut out the Box

On the next page is a box to cut out. Cut out the figure, fold it, and paste the edges together so that you make your own box. You need this box to look at and to draw.

Now, once you have the box together, you will need to find a piece of clear glass or plexiglass or vinyl (like a report cover) and a felt tip pen that you can use to draw on your clear sheet.

Take your box and set it up behind your clear sheet. Then hold the clear, transparent sheet stationary while you trace the box on it. Hold everything very steady. Trace the box exactly as you see it. Keep your eye in one steady position, the box steady, and the clear sheet still. If you don't move any of them, then you can draw the box in correct perspective.

One hint; don't use both eyes. Shut one eye. If you use two eyes, you will get a double image making it difficult to draw. So make sure you shut one eye so as to get one image.

If you move the box up or down or if you move up or down, you see different views of the top and bottom of the box—you see different planes. The view of the surface that you see changes as your eye level changes. This eye level line is called a horizon line. The horizon line is always level and is always at the level of your eye. Thus the view of the top and bottom of the box changes as you move your eye level or horizon line.

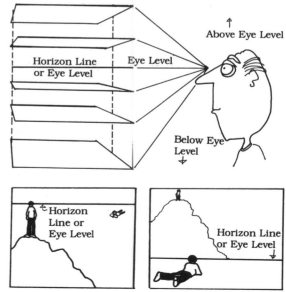

16

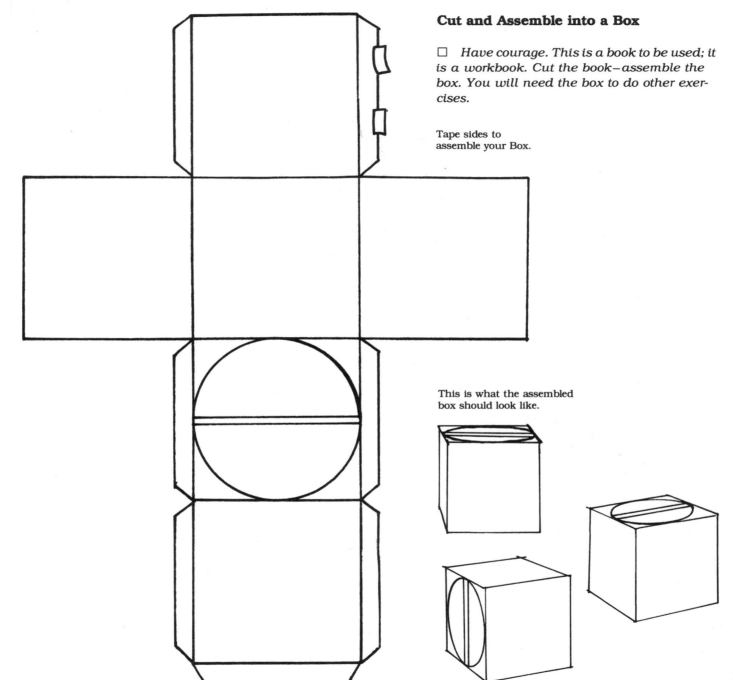

Cut and Assemble into a Box

☐ *Have courage. This is a book to be used; it is a workbook. Cut the book—assemble the box. You will need the box to do other exercises.*

Tape sides to
assemble your Box.

This is what the assembled
box should look like.

17

Carefully study what happens to the
cube. Turn it sideways. Hold it above your
eye. Hold it below your eye, to one side, to the
other side. Note how the surfaces of that cube
appear to change shape as you change the
position of the cube in relation to your eye.

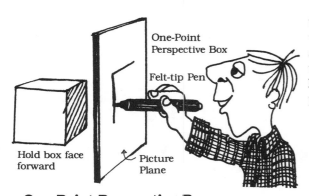

One-Point
Perspective Box

Felt-tip Pen

Hold box face
forward

Picture
Plane

One-Point Perspective Box

If you hold the box directly in front of your eye, you will see one-point perspective. What this means is that all lines appear to converge at one point on the horizon. If you have ever looked down a railroad track, as you stand in the middle of the track, you will notice that the tracks seem to disappear in the distance. They seem to converge at one point far in the distance. This is called one-point perspective. One-point perspective means that parallel lines disappear at one single point on the horizon line in the distance.

There are three different kinds of lines in perspective drawing. One-point perspective has all three of these lines. It has vertical lines, horizontal lines, and perspective lines. Some of

the lines are exactly vertical; they go straight up or straight down and are parallel one to another. Some of the lines are exactly horizontal; they are parallel across the page. Some lines are perspective lines; they converge at a point on the horizon line.

As you draw the box, the surface that you

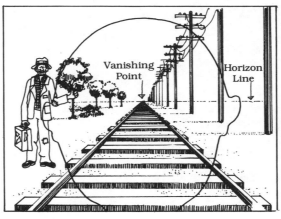

Vanishing Point

Horizon Line

draw it on is called a picture plane. It is the transparent glass surface. The picture plane is your paper if you are drawing the box on a piece of paper. You draw on paper the same as you trace through glass, but instead of looking through the glass (the picture plane) to draw the box, you hold your paper (the picture plane) in front of you and trace that box.

Two-Point Perspective

A second kind of perspective is called two-point perspective. Turn your cube so that you are looking at an edge of that cube. From that edge the sides of the cube seem to get smaller as they go away from your eye. Both sides get smaller. Both sides seem to vanish at *two* different points on the horizon line. For this reason, it is called two-point perspective. Two-point perspective means that from a given edge, parallel lines, like the sides of the cube,

converge at two single points on the horizon line at opposite sides of your paper. Notice how the edges on the Rice Krispie box and the newspaper vending machine seem to get slightly smaller as they go away from you.

Extends toward a single Vanishing Point on the left

Extends toward a single Vanishing Point on the right

19

Three-Point Perspective

The third kind of perspective drawing is three-point perspective. What happens here is that lines appear to converge at three given points either to the sides of the picture plane or at the top or bottom of the page, depending upon where your eye level line is. Look at the corner of the building. As the sides of the building go away from you, the two parallel edges create lines that will disappear at a point on the horizon line. As you look up at the building you will notice that the vertical lines that go up appear to get closer and closer at the top so that they would eventually disappear at a point high above the building. This is three-point perspective.

The photo below is a three-point perspective view of a box of cereal.

The Three Kinds of Perspective

One-Point Perspective
Side of box against glass
3 kinds of lines—
vertical lines,
horizontal lines,
perspective lines

Two-Point Perspective
Edge of box against glass
2 kinds of lines—
vertical lines,
perspective lines

Three-Point Perspective
Corner of box against glass
1 kind of line—
perspective lines

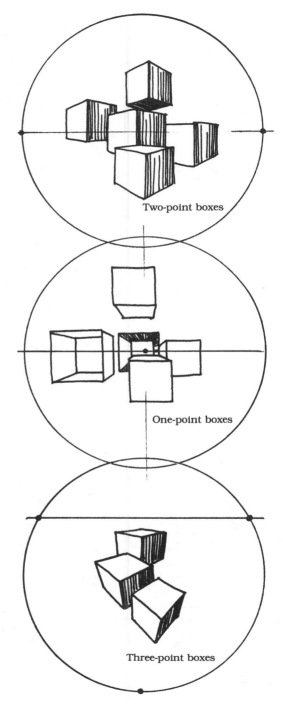

Two-point boxes

One-point boxes

Three-point boxes

Recognizing a Square in Perspective

You need to develop a critical eye so that you can easily see if a cube is drawn in correct perspective. Below are some lines that are three sides of a square. The fourth side has not been drawn in.

☐ *You draw the fourth side so that these squares show accurate perspective. Slide a straight edge along until the square appears visually correct to you. Then, draw the line.*

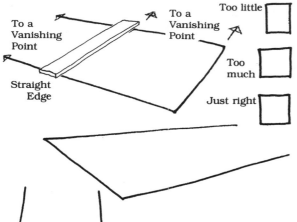

Key Principles of Perspective

Here are some of the key principles to remember when drawing boxes in perspective:

1. Perspective lines converge at a vanishing point.
2. The horizon line is always horizontal.
3. The nearest angle is 90° or greater.
4. The sides of a cube are proportional to a square.

Some common errors happen when you learn to drawn cubes. Let me tell you just a few of them to watch for.

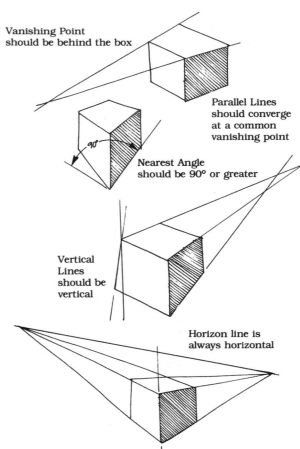

21

Recognizing a Cube

Some of the cubes below are drawn incorrectly. What is wrong with them?

☐ *Draw over the cubes so that you fix what is wrong. (The cubes have at least one of four things wrong: (1) convergence (2) horizon line, (3) nearest angle, (4) incorrect proportion. Each cube may have more than one thing wrong with it.)*

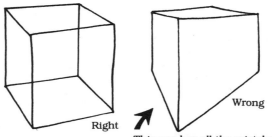

Right   Wrong

This one has all the mistakes. You may want to draw the hidden edge lines of the cube to help you determine what is wrong.

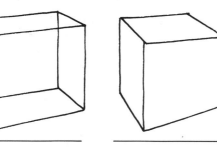 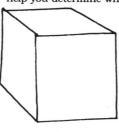 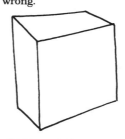

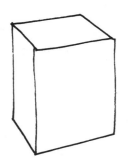 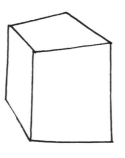 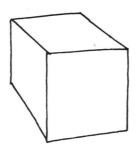 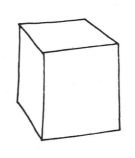

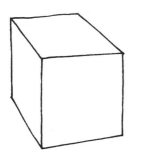 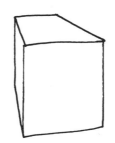 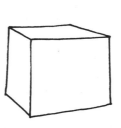 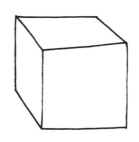

An Explanation

Below is a circle with a lot of different cubes drawn in that circle. The line going straight across is your horizon line. Above or below the horizon line the cubes begin to distort because of the perspective drawing. All of these cubes are drawn in two-point perspective. Whenever you draw things in perspective, you will find it helpful to imagine that you are drawing within the limits of a circle. If you draw things beyond that imaginary circle, then the cubes appear to be so distorted that they don't seem real. So you need to draw within that imaginary cicrle.

Two-Point Box in Perspective

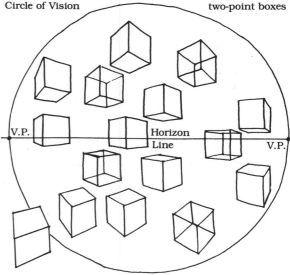

Circle of Vision   two-point boxes

V.P.   Horizon Line   V.P.

Boxes outside of circle appear distorted

Keep all boxes inside circle

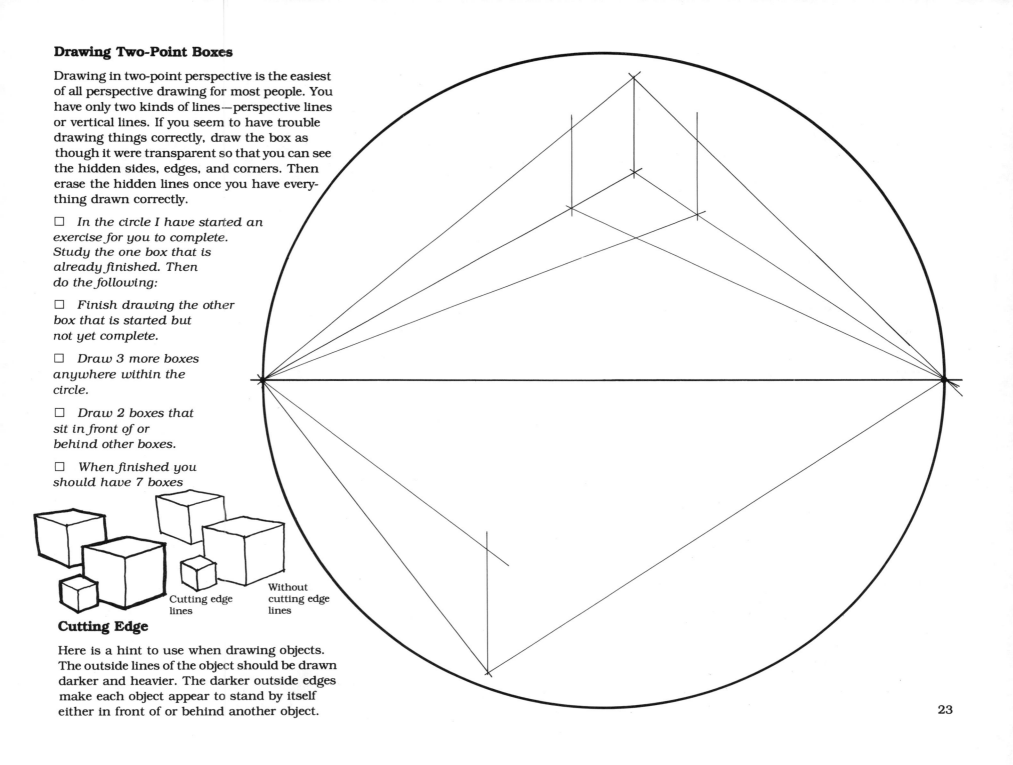

Drawing Two-Point Boxes

Drawing in two-point perspective is the easiest of all perspective drawing for most people. You have only two kinds of lines—perspective lines or vertical lines. If you seem to have trouble drawing things correctly, draw the box as though it were transparent so that you can see the hidden sides, edges, and corners. Then erase the hidden lines once you have everything drawn correctly.

☐ *In the circle I have started an exercise for you to complete. Study the one box that is already finished. Then do the following:*

☐ *Finish drawing the other box that is started but not yet complete.*

☐ *Draw 3 more boxes anywhere within the circle.*

☐ *Draw 2 boxes that sit in front of or behind other boxes.*

☐ *When finished you should have 7 boxes*

Cutting edge lines

Without cutting edge lines

Cutting Edge

Here is a hint to use when drawing objects. The outside lines of the object should be drawn darker and heavier. The darker outside edges make each object appear to stand by itself either in front of or behind another object.

23

Drawing One-Point Boxes

You have three kinds of lines in one-point perspective—vertical lines, horizontal lines, and perspective lines. If you seem to have trouble drawing things correctly, draw the box as though it were transparent so that you can see the hidden sides, edges, and corners. Then erase the hidden lines, once you have everything drawn correctly, thus leaving a solid box.

☐ *In the circle I have started another exercise for you to complete. Do the following:*

☐ *Draw 2 more boxes anywhere within the circle.*

☐ *Draw 2 boxes that sit in front of or behind other boxes.*

☐ *When finished, you should have 5 boxes.*

A Distortion Problem

In one-point perspective the farther away from the central vanishing point, the closer to the outer edge of the circle, the more distortion. With one-point perspective this distortion that occurs when you near the outer limits of the circle is more pronounced than with two and three-point perspective.

Drawing Three-Point Boxes

There is only one kind of line in three-point perspective—perspective lines. Draw the box as though it were transparent so that you can see the hidden sides, edges, and corners if you have trouble drawing things correctly. Once you have everything drawn correctly, erase the hidden lines.

☐ *In the circle I have started another exercise for you to complete. Study the one box that is already finished. Then do the following:*

☐ *Draw 3 more boxes anywhere within the circle.*

☐ *Draw 2 boxes that sit in front of or behind other boxes.*

☐ *When finished you should have at least 5 boxes.*

Upside Down

The boxes within this circle will look like you're looking down on them. To reverse the point of view simply turn the book upside down. The boxes will then look like you are underneath them.

Dividing a Square

The diagonal lines drawn from corner to corner of a square cross in the exact middle of that square. A line drawn from the middle of the square to the vanishing point bisects the edge at midpoint. Now draw a line from the corner through the midpoint of the side. This line from the corner through the midpoint of the side will cross the bottom line of the square, giving you the location at the far corner of the next square. See the illustration below. This principle is used to help divide a square into equal segments or to enlarge a square in equal segments.

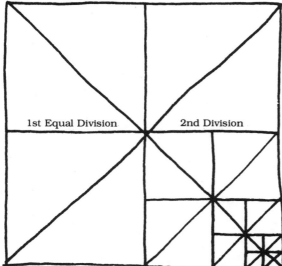

1st Equal Division   2nd Division

Below is a square drawn in perspective. You are above the square looking down on it. Using the diagonal to divide the square applies in perspective also.

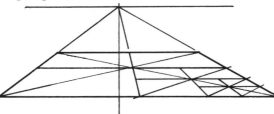

☐ *Here are some examples of cubes and squares. Draw diagonals so as to cut these squares and cubes directly in half. I have divided one cube to show you how it is done. Divide the squares and cubes below—divide them in half, then divide one side in quarters. You will need to draw the hidden edges (sides of the cubes away from you that you don't see) of the cube in order to know where to divide it.*

Use diagonal lines to locate the center of objects.

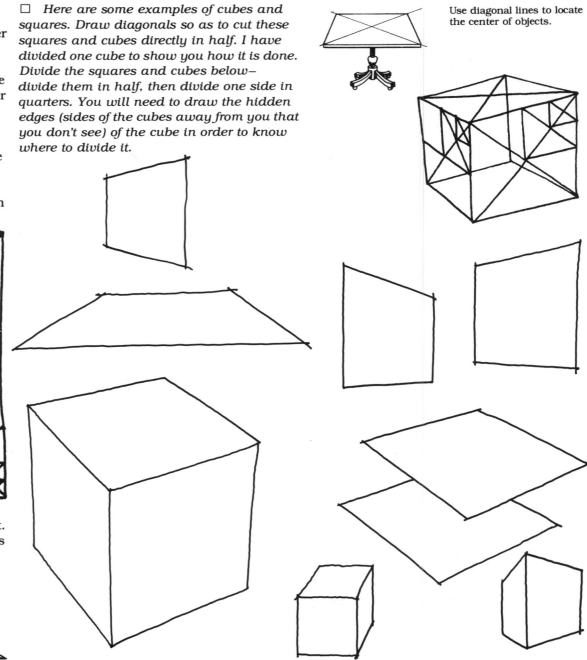

26

A Unit of Measurement

A cube can act as a standard of measurement. The cubes drawn below are all the same size, but they appear to be different sizes because of the surroundings—the man, the lady, the foot. These different cubes can act as different units of measurement. The cube can be one inch, one foot, a five-foot section, one city block, or one mile.

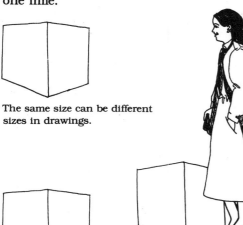

The same size can be different sizes in drawings.

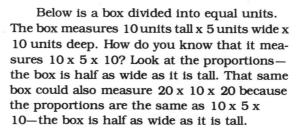

Below is a box divided into equal units. The box measures 10 units tall x 5 units wide x 10 units deep. How do you know that it measures 10 x 5 x 10? Look at the proportions— the box is half as wide as it is tall. That same box could also measure 20 x 10 x 20 because the proportions are the same as 10 x 5 x 10—the box is half as wide as it is tall.

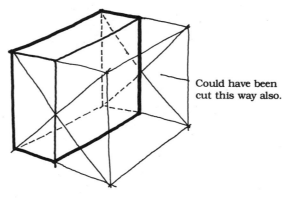

Could have been cut this way also.

☐ *Divide the cubes below. Figure the proportions and divide accordingly. Use cubes as units of measurement. Divide the cubes to get correct proportions.*

The same size can be different sizes in drawings. You need not be exact. Estimate as well as you can.

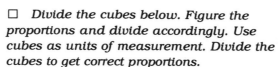

☐ *Draw this one 5 x 5 x 10.*

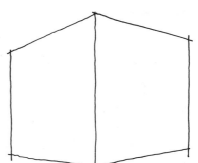

☐ *Draw this one 10 x 10 x 5.*

☐ *Draw this one 1 x 1 x 0.5*

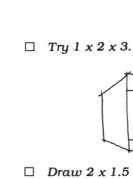

☐ *Try 1 x 2 x 3.*

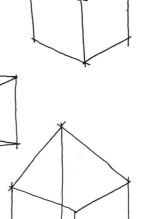

☐ *Draw 2 x 1.5 x 1.*

☐ *And last, draw this one 100 x 100 x 75.* 27

Adding Squares

This same principle of using diagonal lines to find the exact middle of the sides of a box also enables you to draw more than one square in perspective. First, you find the exact middle of the square. Then you extend a line from the corner through the middle of the far side. Where that line intersects, the bottom perspective line shows you the length of the next square in perspective.

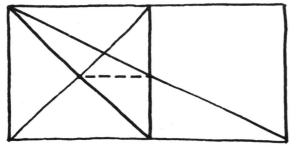

Squares drawn in perspective appear to diminish in size. You can find the correct rate that they diminish by drawing the diagonal lines to find the center of the far edge of the square. Then draw another diagonal line that goes from the corner of the square directly through the midpoint of the edge and on down to where it finds the bottom corner of the next square. Once you have learned this principle you can apply it to draw many things.

Below is drawn one square in perspective. Use this principle to help you determine where the next square in succession should be located.

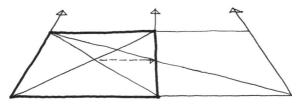

A sequence of adding squares to make a drawing

☐ *Add squares to the following drawings. Add as many as you can.*

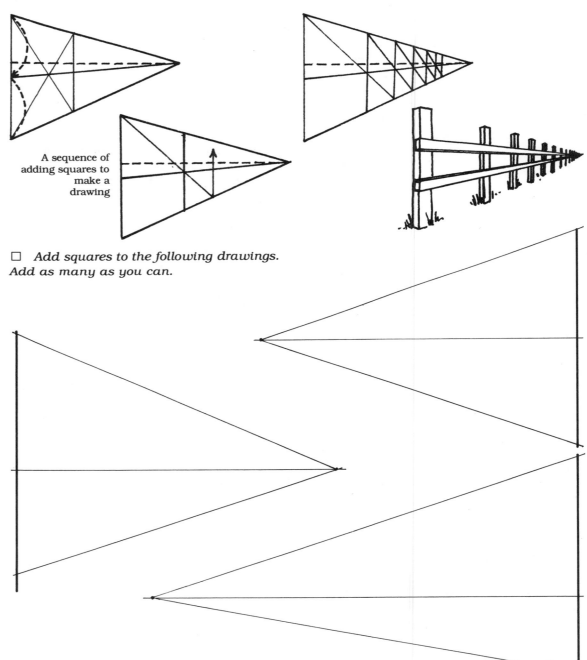

Multiplying Squares and Boxes

These squares that you draw in perspective can become cubes. The same principles that apply to the square apply to a cube or to a box. Just stack cubes upon one another or next to one another to draw larger and more complicated objects.

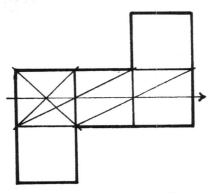

The same method that works in two dimensions will also work in three dimensions.

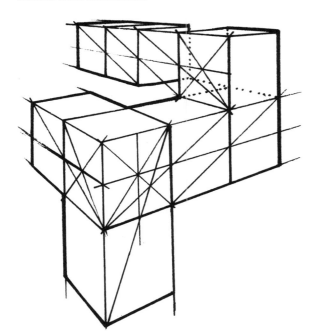

Drawing in Perspective

The following is a summary of this process used to draw other squares, boxes, or cubes in correct proportion:

1. First, use the diagonal to find the center of the side.
2. Draw a line from the center of the side to the vanishing point—this bisects the far side exactly in half.
3. Draw a line from the corner through the center of the far side to where it intersects with the bottom perspective line of the box.
4. This intersection between the diagonal through the side to the bottom gives you the size of the next square or box.

Out of One Make Many

☐ *Draw 3 cubes in every direction from the one shown here (in front, behind, above, below, to the right side, to the left side). Lay tracing paper over the illustration—draw a multiple cubic structure.*

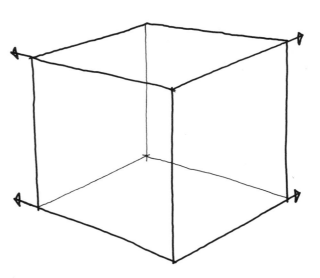

Another Way to Multiply a Square

Another principle that you'll find useful is that diagonal lines converge at a single vanishing point. The illustration below demonstrates how this works. The boxes must be equal in size (squares in this case). The sides of the box must be parallel—the bottoms line up in the illustration below. As you can see, the diagonal lines are all **parallel**. If you draw these diagonal lines in perspective, the diagonal lines converge at a common vanishing point.

You can use this knowledge to help you quickly draw things in perspective. If you easily can determine diagonal lines of boxes you can then find the far corner and can add more boxes quickly.

In the lower left hand corner is an illustration of many cubes drawn in perspective. It becomes easy to add more cubes to this because, since the diagonal lines converge at a vanishing point, it is easy to determine where the corners of the additional cubes will be located.

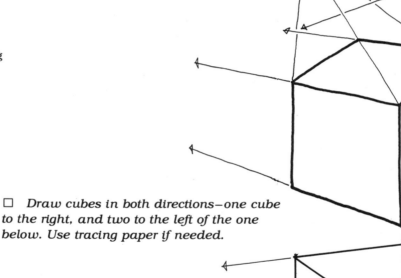

Parallel lines will converge at a common vanishing point when drawn in perspective.

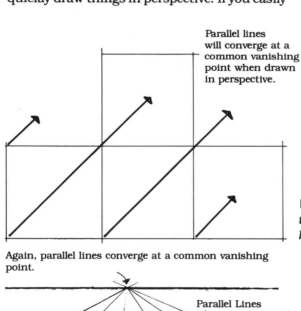

Again, parallel lines converge at a common vanishing point.

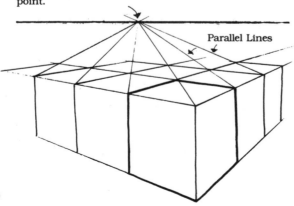

☐ *Draw cubes in both directions—one cube to the right, and two to the left of the one below. Use tracing paper if needed.*

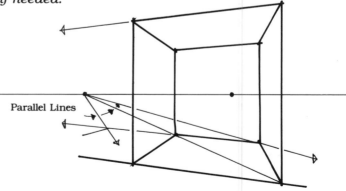

Vertically Adding Boxes

Parallel lines (sides of a flat surface that sets at an angle such as a roof top or open box lid) converge at a single point. You could use this knowledge to help you draw the rooftop of a building. The lines that form the side of that roof, when extended, converge at a vanishing point directly above the vanishing point on the horizon line. This point above the horizon line is called a "trace." You will find it useful to know that these lines do converge at a point above or below the vanishing point on the horizon line.

☐ Add two cubes in every direction from the drawing below–2 above, 2 behind, 2 in front of, 2 below, 2 on each side. You will probably find it easier to trace the box than to try to do it all on this page.

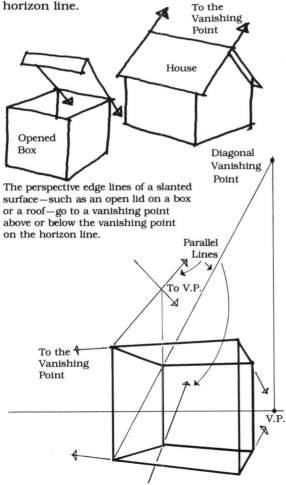

The perspective edge lines of a slanted surface—such as an open lid on a box or a roof—go to a vanishing point above or below the vanishing point on the horizon line.

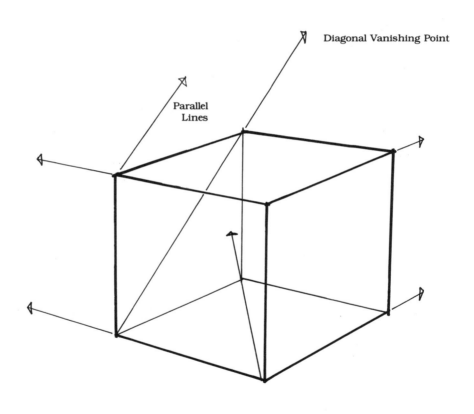

Don't let all the lines confuse you—it's the same thing repeated over and over again.

Assorted Boxes

You will need to draw different sized boxes. To this point we have concentrated on cubes—boxes with equal-sized sides. You can draw odd-sized boxes by putting two or more cubes together to help you draw the different sized boxes.

On this page I have drawn some examples of assorted-sized boxes. I have also left room for you to draw other boxes with instructions as to exactly how your boxes should be drawn. Use the space to practice the principles shown here.

The goal you should be striving for is to draw accurate perspective without having to draw all the hidden sides, vanishing points, and converging lines. You should become so familiar with how things *should* look when drawn correctly that you can do it right the first time.

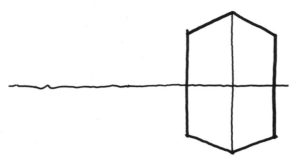

☐ *Draw a 1 x 2 x 1 box using two-point perspective at eye level.*

☐ *Draw a 5 x 5 x 10 box using one-point perspective below eye level so that you are looking inside.*

☐ *Draw a 2.5 x 2 x 3 box using two-point perspective below eye level.*

☐ *Draw a 5 x 7 x 9 box using three-point perspective at eye level.*

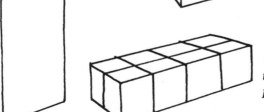

☐ *Draw a 2 x 4 x 1 box using one-point perspective below eye level.*

☐ *Draw a 6.5 x 5 x 3 box using three-point perspective at eye level.*

☐ *Draw a 2 x 2 x 5 box with an open top so that you can see inside using one-point perspective at eye level.*

☐ *Choose 2 or more boxes that you want to draw. Decide the eye level and the perspective you want to see. Draw them.*

Different Views

Once you have learned how to draw boxes and squares, the next thing is to learn to get different objects from these boxes.

When drawing buildings for architecture, you show different views of the proposed building. You usually show a front view, a side view, and a top view. All these views are as if you placed your building within a glass box and then traced the appropriate view. If you look down, directly on the top of your box, you see the top view of the building. If you look at one side, you see the side view, and so on.

You need to learn how to convert those three different views into a three-dimensional object. Remember that these different views are as though you were peeling away the sides of a box with an object drawn on the sides of that box. They are flat views of a three-dimensional object.

☐ *Three views are converted into a perspective drawing here for you. You proceed to draw the three-dimensional image of the other views on the next page.*

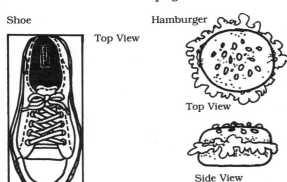

Shoe

Top View

Front View

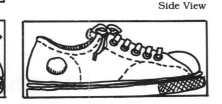

☐ *Draw the top, front, and side views of a table.*

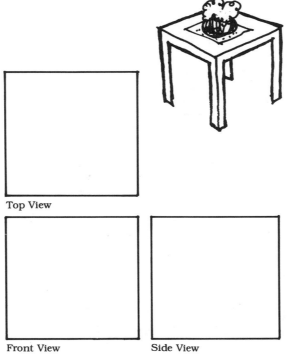

Top View

Front View　　　　Side View

Place the object inside a transparent box. The views are drawn on the sides of the box. Then the box is unfolded.

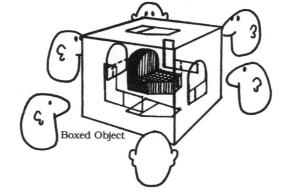

Boxed Object

Hamburger

Top View

Side View

Side View

When it is completely unfolded, you see the different views of the object.

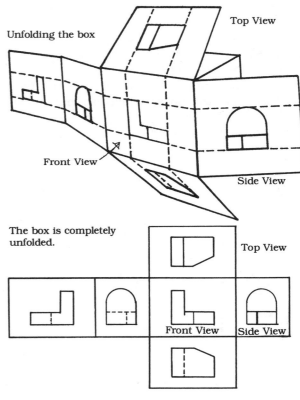

Unfolding the box

Top View

Front View

Side View

The box is completely unfolded.

Top View

Front View　　Side View

☐ *You draw the views of the object shown here.*

Top

Front　　　　　Side

33

Visualizing the Object

This page contains the top, front, and side views of many different objects. You need to learn how to visualize those objects as they really look—you need to recognize the three-dimensional object by seeing the two-dimensional top, front, and side views.

☐ *The three-dimensional view of the first object is shown. You draw the three-dimensional view of the other objects. You may want to draw them on separate sheets.*

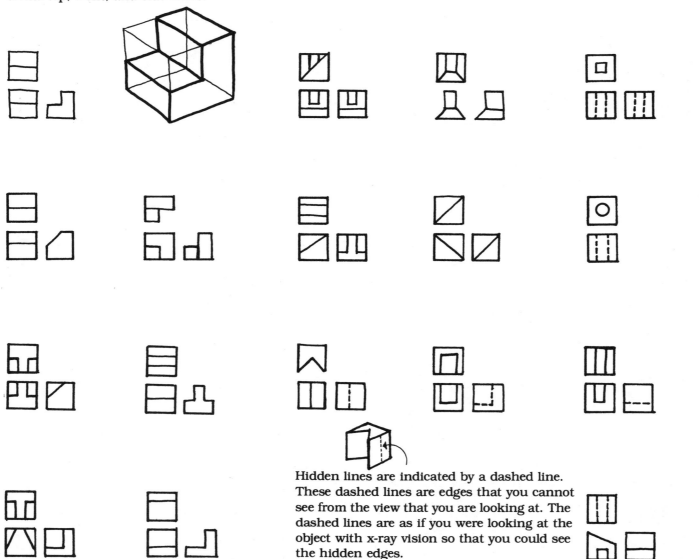

Hidden lines are indicated by a dashed line. These dashed lines are edges that you cannot see from the view that you are looking at. The dashed lines are as if you were looking at the object with x-ray vision so that you could see the hidden edges.

34

Complicated Objects

You can draw complex and complicated objects by using more than one box to help you. Refer back a few pages where using more than one box to draw odd-shaped boxes is discussed.

☐ *Draw the 3-dimensional view of the objects shown here.*

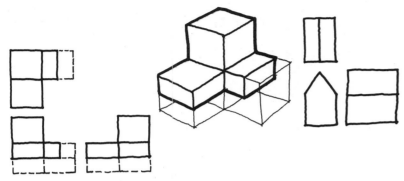

The dotted lines here indicate the edges of multiple boxes stacked together and enclosing the object.

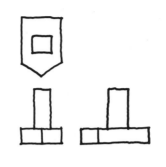

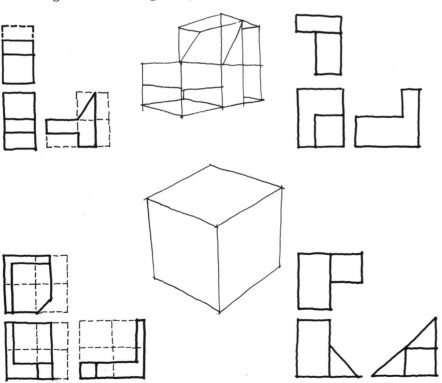

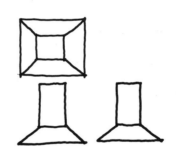

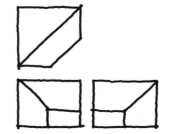

Cube Shelving

Shown here is a method of building shelves called abstracta. It consists of tubing that connects at the corners to form boxes. These cubes, when stacked in different configurations, form shelving for display.

☐ *Lay a piece of tracing paper over the drawing below. You evolve the drawing on the tracing paper. Draw at least 7 more cubes of shelves to create your own Abstracta display case.*

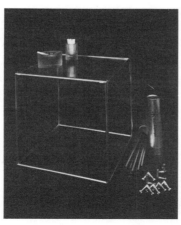

This shelving is just a series of boxes.

Draw objects sitting on the shelves.

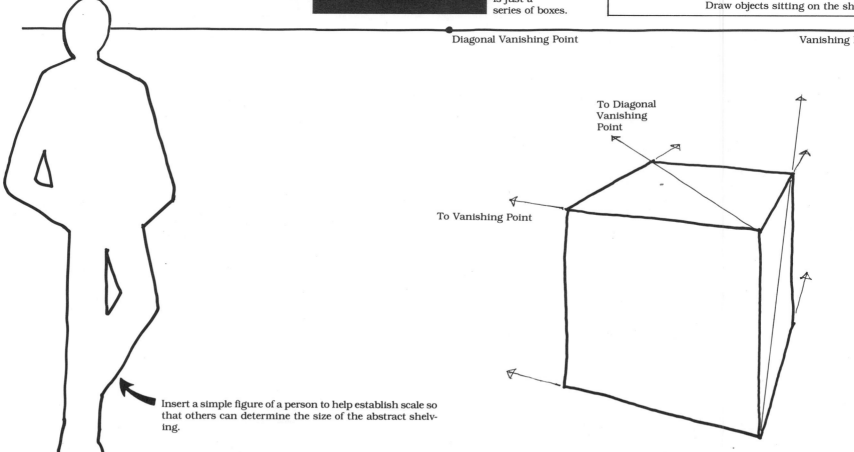

Diagonal Vanishing Point

Vanishing Point

To Diagonal Vanishing Point

To Vanishing Point

Insert a simple figure of a person to help establish scale so that others can determine the size of the abstract shelving.

Drawing a Chair

You've learned how to draw cubes and squares and how to visualize things that sit within transparent imaginative cubes. Now I'll show you how to draw objects by using the cube method. If you can draw a cube, then you can draw other objects. For example, I arrived at a chair by beginning first with a cube and then erasing the lines of the cube so that all that remains is the chair.

☐ *Draw 5 chairs. I've started some. You complete the ones already started, then draw other chairs until you have 5 complete chairs.*

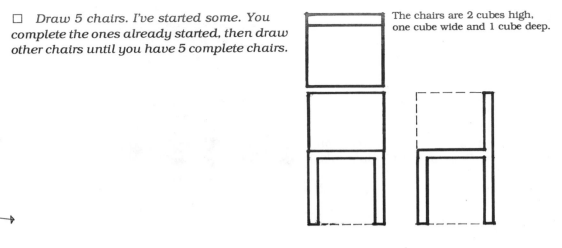

The chairs are 2 cubes high, one cube wide and 1 cube deep.

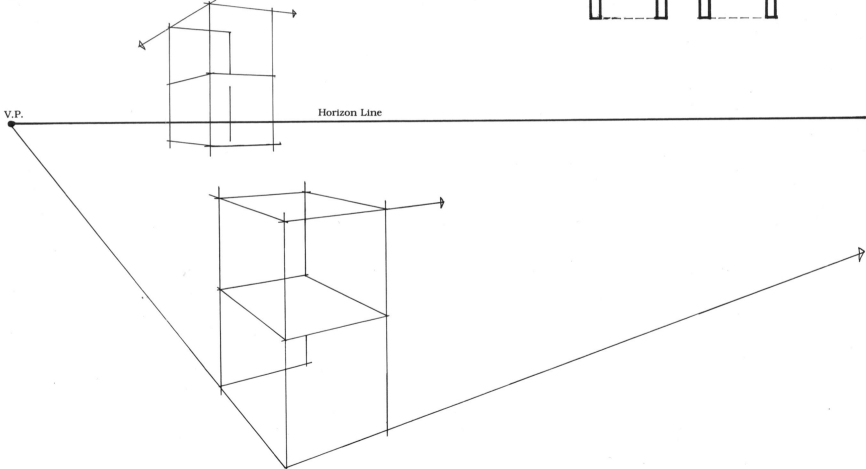

V.P.

Horizon Line

Other Kinds of Chairs

All of the chairs shown here are made the same way as the basic simple chair. First draw a box and then place the chair inside of that box. Get some magazines so that you can find a variety of chairs to draw.

☐ *Draw at least 3 other chairs from the pictures you have found in the magazines. Use the box method for drawing the chairs.*

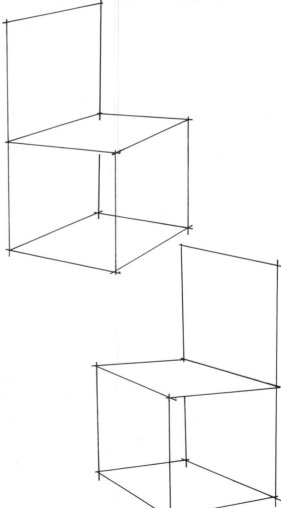

Drawing a Sofa

A sofa is an extended chair. Drawing a sofa is like stacking three or four chairs next to one another.

☐ *Using the same principle of multiple boxes to draw extended chairs, draw a sofa.*

☐ *Draw a different sofa using the same principle of different cubes stacked next to each other.*

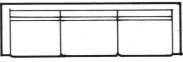

Top View

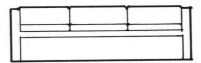

Front View

Side View

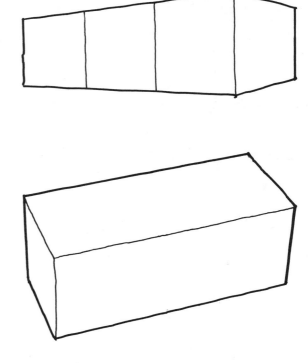

Steps in drawing a sofa

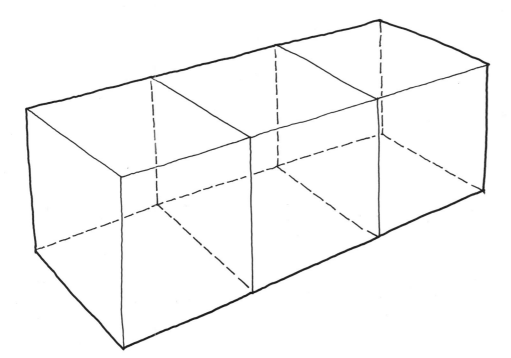

Creating Objects from Boxes

Shown here are some basic shaped boxes that have been converted into a variety of objects. By cutting away parts of the basic box shape you can create finished drawings of items that do not appear to have evolved from a box in the beginning.

☐ *Draw the object that is asked for. I've drawn the box–you finish the object.*

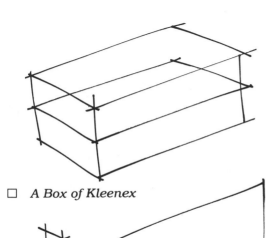

☐ *A Box of Kleenex*

☐ *A suitcase*

☐ *A bed*

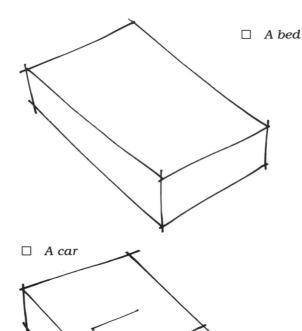

☐ *A car*

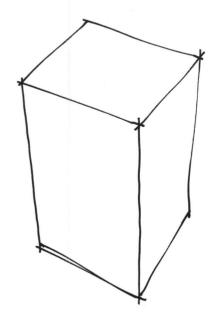

☐ *A tall building with a helicopter landing pad on the roof*

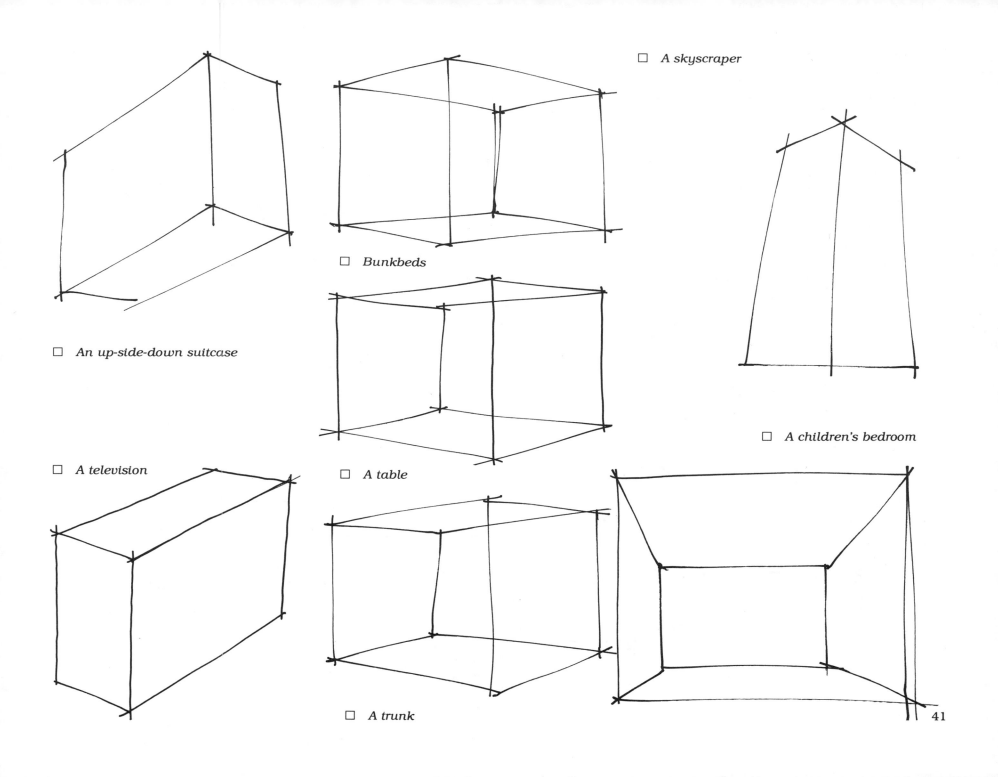

☐ A skyscraper

☐ Bunkbeds

☐ An up-side-down suitcase

☐ A children's bedroom

☐ A television

☐ A table

☐ A trunk

41

Drawing a Building

Drawing the exterior of a building is accomplished by using the same principle as drawing previous objects. You stack different squares or different cubes next to each other to form a basic building. Use the principles of diagonal lines to find how to correctly stack your cubes in perspective. Then, you can create the different angles and views and surfaces for the building. Shown here is a building I constructed using cubes to help draw the final view of that building. It was done simply by extending cubes. We started with one cube and then extended cubes in different directions to get the other sides and surfaces of the building.

☐ *Place a piece of tracing paper over the building shown here. Trace and finish the drawing—include windows, doors, trees, etc. to complete the drawing.*

The dimensions of the building are 6 units long by 2 units wide by 2 units tall.

42

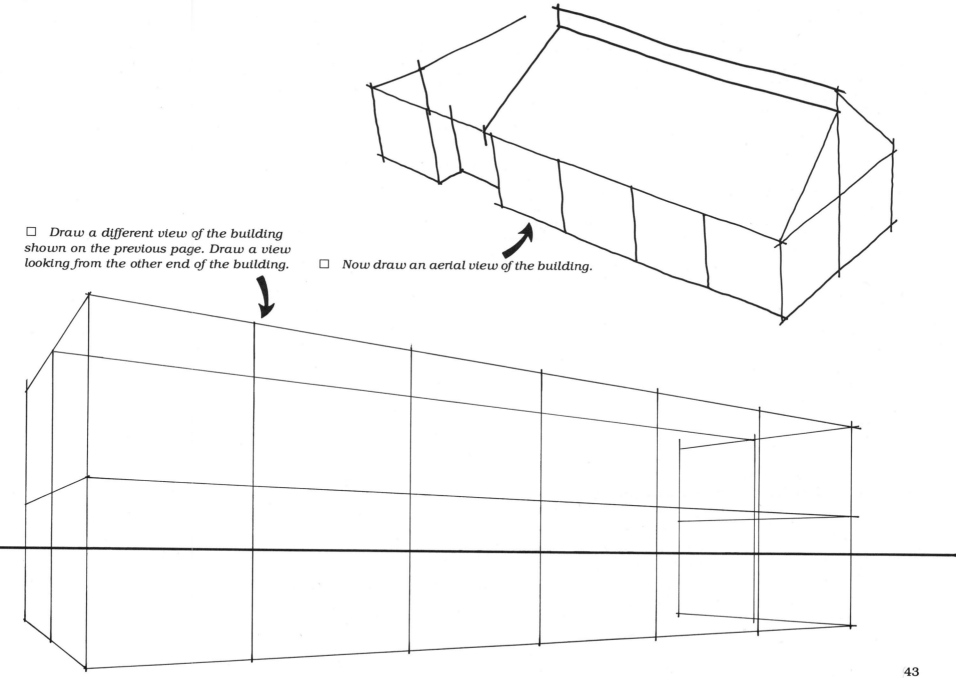

☐ Draw a different view of the building shown on the previous page. Draw a view looking from the other end of the building.

☐ Now draw an aerial view of the building.

43

Drawing Interiors

In architecture and interior design you need to learn how to draw objects within a room. Drawing objects within a room starts with a floor plan (a top view of the room). It is very simple. Use boxes and cubes, as I've shown you, to make the different furniture or objects for the room. Then use the top view to place everything where it goes.

Below are the steps for creating the interior of the room shown here. Study each step until you understand exactly what has been done. The whole process looks complicated, but it isn't. The process looks time consuming,

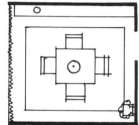

Top View or Plan View

 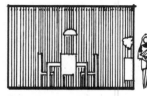 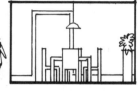

Side View or Elevation Side View or Elevation Side View or Elevation

The dimensions of the room are 12 x 12 x 8.

but it isn't when compared to other drawing methods. It took only a few minutes to draw what is shown here. These are my thumbnail sketches of the interior shown full-size on the following page.

Draw a square;
it is 12 feet square

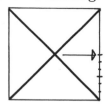

Find the midpoint of the side

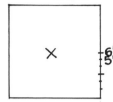

Divide the side into equal units—6 below the mid-point

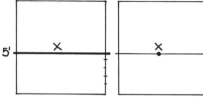

Find eye level—usually the 5 foot mark

Draw the horizon line and vanishing point

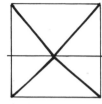

Draw the perspective lines

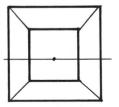

Estimate the depth of your 12 x 12 x 8 room.

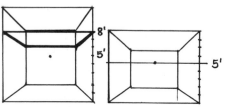

Lower the ceiling to the 8 foot mark

Put in the ceiling—erase the excess

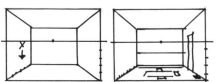

Put in marks for depth measurement—use the diagonals to find the midpoint

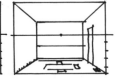

Draw views on the outside surfaces

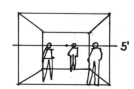

Put in human figures to establish scale

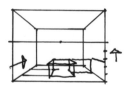

Project views to draw objects

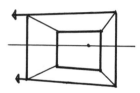

The room can be made more interesting in 2-point perspective

Remember the basic principles in dealing with boxes. In most complex drawings they are just repeated over and over again.

□ *Place tracing paper over the drawing. Finish and refine the room. Put paintings on the walls, include lamps, refine the roughed in furniture, add windows, etc.*

□ *Draw another point of view of the same room. Look in at the same room from one of the other walls.*

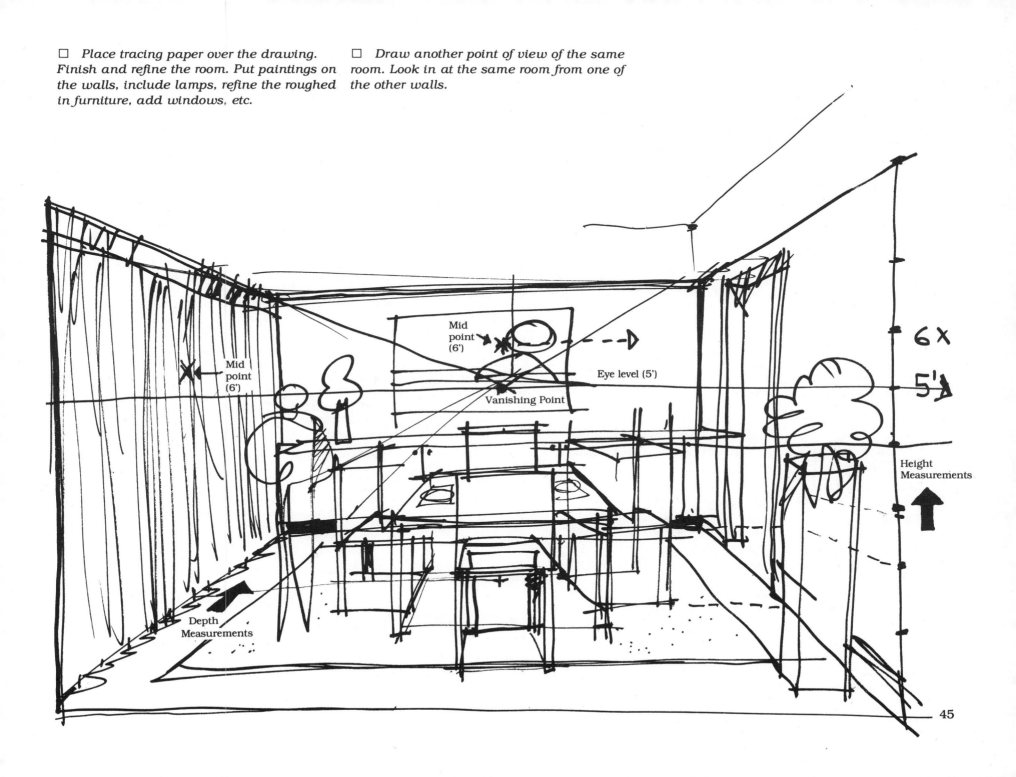

Mid point (6')

Mid point (6')

Eye level (5')

Vanishing Point

Depth Measurements

6 X

5'

Height Measurements

45

Grids

The Grid Method is a way of enlarging, reducing, or putting in perspective any object that you draw. Lay a grid over your drawing. Then make a new grid apart from your drawing. To finish, transfer your drawing square by square from the old grid to the new one.

This is how it's done. Take your original object and place over the top of it a grid system of equal size squares.

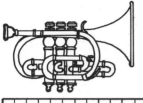

Original drawing

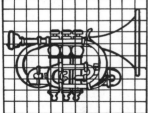

Grid overlay

Make a new grid and transfer your drawing one square at a time.

You can enlarge or reduce the object by using the grid. If you want the copy to be larger than the original. Use larger squares for the new grid. Copy, square by square, what you see in the original. Since the second grid is larger, the finished copy will be larger than the original. In a like manner, you can reduce something by using smaller squares than in the original grid.

If you want to draw an object in perspective, the grid that you transfer onto should be drawn in perspective. The illustration here shows how it's done.

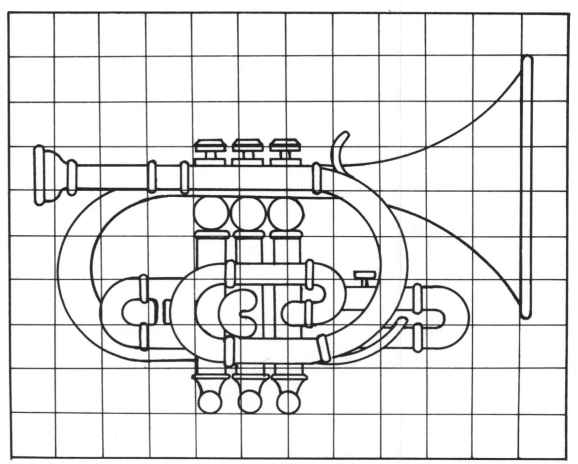

Enlarged grid with drawing in place

Grid drawn in perspective with drawing in place

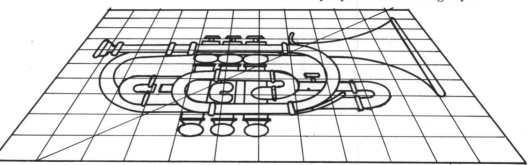

Drawing Buildings and Landscapes

You will find it very helpful to have the grid method for drawing buildings and landscapes. By superimposing a grid over views of a building, or landscape, you can transfer the building easily onto a new surface. Here's how its done

1. Place a grid over the original drawing
2. Lay a piece of tracing paper over a new grid
3. Transfer the old drawing one square at a time

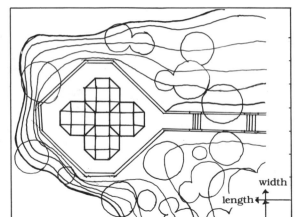

width

length

Since you are drawing on a tracing paper with the new grid underneath, your final drawing will not show the grid. The drawing will be accurate because of the grid system used, but it will not be apparent from the final drawing that you used a grid to accomplish the task.

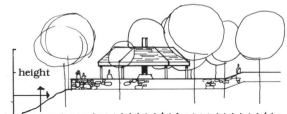

height

☐ *Lay tracing paper over this grid and transfer the small views of the park structure onto it in a perspective drawing. But first draw a grid of equal squares over the small views.*

47

Putting Other Things in the Box

Up to now I have shown you how to put other things in a box—cone, circle, cube, and cylinder. Here I'll show you how to use the box to draw a sphere. Once you learn to draw the sphere you will have knowledge of all the basic shapes that are so important to accurate drawing.

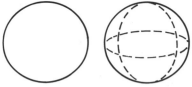

Many people think that drawing a sphere is like drawing a circle. That is not exactly correct. A circle is two dimensional while a sphere is three dimensional. Here's an example of the difference between a circle and a sphere:

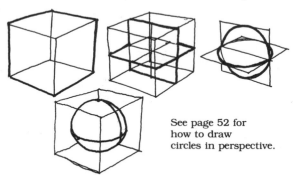

See page 52 for how to draw circles in perspective.

Here's how you draw a sphere:

1. Draw a cube.
2. Draw two dissecting planes that cut the cube in half both vertically and horizontally.
3. Draw ellipses within the planes in the square. Touch the mid points of the squares within the cube.

☐ *Draw what it would look like if 1/4 of the sphere were cut away. Draw a different point of view than shown above.*

☐ *Cut 1/2 of a sphere away. Again draw a different point of view than shown above.*

Basic Shapes

All objects are made up from four basic shapes—cube, sphere, cylinder, or cone. You begin with a cube and from that cube you can extract a sphere, or you can extract a cylinder, or you can extract a cone shape. These four—the cube, sphere, cylinder and cone—are the basic shapes that can be used to draw anything. If you will learn to see objects as basic shapes, you will more easily be able to draw the different objects.

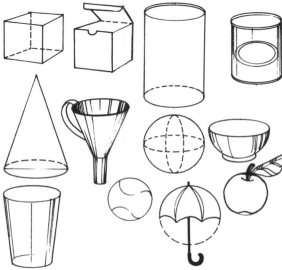

A Point To Remember

At least one time in your drawing experiences you will encounter an instance when your drawing just "doesn't look right." When this happens go back to basics. First construct your drawing using basic shapes. Use cubes, spheres, cylinders, and cones to give form to the object. Then evolve these basic shapes until you create the drawing that you are looking for. When problems crop up, go back to basic shapes and start over. I have to do it often to get my drawings to work out. It will help you also.

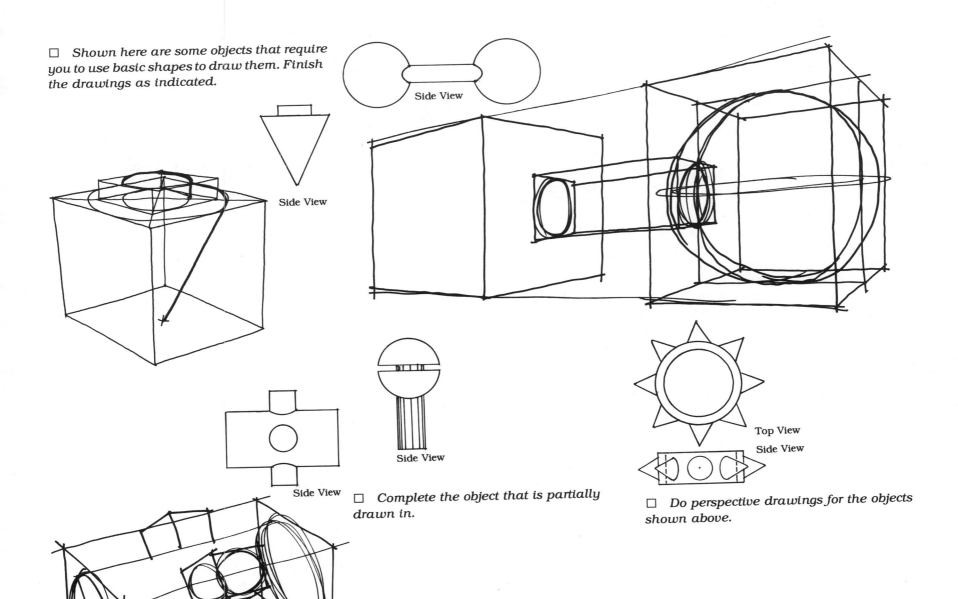

□ *Shown here are some objects that require you to use basic shapes to draw them. Finish the drawings as indicated.*

Side View

Side View

Side View

Side View

Side View

Top View

Side View

□ *Complete the object that is partially drawn in.*

□ *Do perspective drawings for the objects shown above.*

49

Drawing with Basic Shapes

Let me give you two exercises to learn to draw the different basic shapes. Here I have drawn a machine that converts spheres into cubes. The machine starts with spheres, small balls, and through seven different steps gradually changes those balls back into cubes.

☐ *You do the same thing. Choose two basic shapes and create a machine that changes one shape into the other. In drawing the machine you should use all of the basic shapes for the different parts of the machine. Your machine should use seven steps to convert one basic shape into the other. You'll know that your machine is correct if someone else can accurately describe the conversion process that you have attempted to illustrate.*

☐ *Draw a birds-eye-view of where you are now. Use basic shapes to draw the different forms. Label all the streets, buildings, and/or rooms shown in your drawing.*

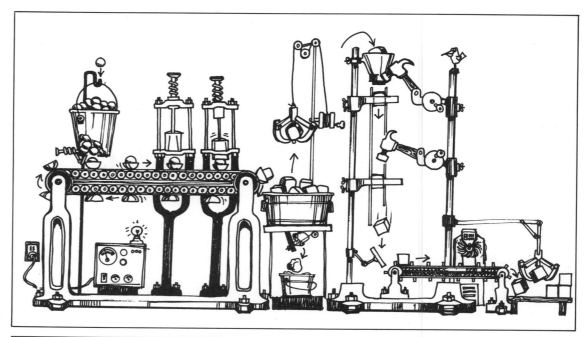

50   These two drawings are just examples of student work.
There may be better ways to do it for you.

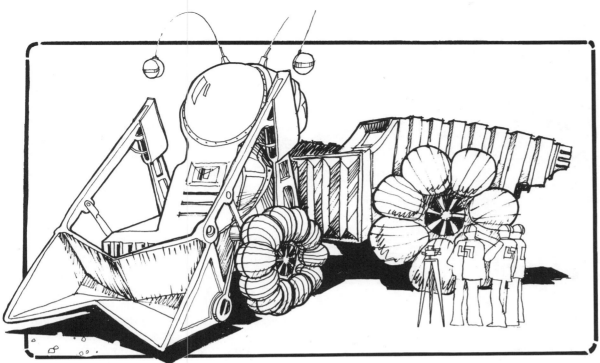

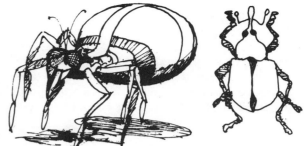

Half Insect—Half Machine

☐ Another exercise for using different basic shapes would be to create a half-insect, half-machine. Combine the two elements to make one machine that is half-machine, half-insect. You may wish to refer to books about insects and photos of heavy machinery to get ideas for your insect-machine.

Furniture/Appliance

☐ Draw a piece of furniture or an appliance. Use all the basic shapes of a sphere, cube, cylinder, and cone to create your new furniture. Your designs will probably be more fantasy than reality. These are new, modern, far-out objects that you are creating.

☐ Draw a toaster from a cone, a cube, and 2 spheres.

☐ Draw a radio from 2 spheres and a cylinder.

☐ Draw a chair from 2 spheres and a cube.

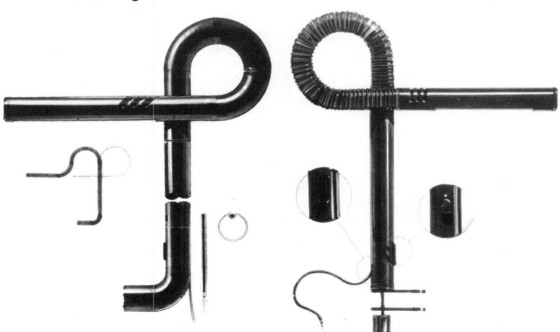

This is a light using a series of cones.

Ellipse

An ellipse is a circle drawn in perspective. Circular objects that you see in real life—tires, cups, coins, saucers, discs and so on—appear as an ellipse because you see them in perspective most of the time.

Drawing An Ellipse

To draw an ellipse is an easy process. First, draw a circle inside a square. Draw diagonal lines from the corners. Draw lines from the midpoint of the sides of the square. Plot a point 1/3 in from the corner on the diagonal. Now draw a gentle curve that passes through the points 1/3 in on the diagonals and touches all four midpoints of the sides of the square. You have drawn a perfect circle.

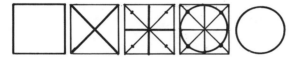

The process for drawing an ellipse is exactly the same as for the circle. But this time you will draw the square in perspective. The circle in the square, when drawn in perspective, is an ellipse.

The Minor Axis

The minor axis is the narrowest diameter of an ellipse. It is always in the direction of a pin if it is pushed through the center. Also it is the direction of the axle of a wheel or the shaft on a cylinder or the center of a cone. Keep that in mind and it will eliminate a lot of distortion problems.

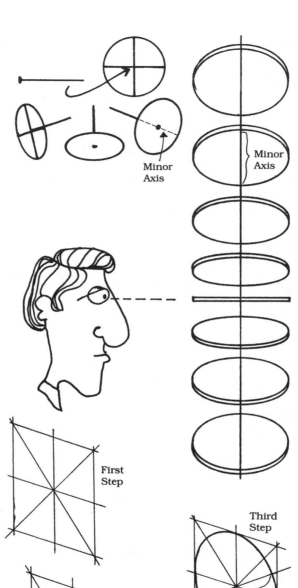

A Circle in Perspective

Take a coin or some other perfectly round object and hold it level with your eye. If you look straight on that object you will see that it is exactly flat—it's a straight line. As you raise the object up you see different views of that object. You see elongated circles. Those elongated circles are ellipses, circles seen in perspective. Raise it up above your eye or down below your eye and look at it—look at the visual changes that occur.

☐ *Remember that cube you cut out and assembled previously? Find it. The cube has a circle drawn on one side. Cut out the circle. (If you can't find the cube, draw a circle on a piece of paper and cut it out.) Through the center point of the circle draw two perpendicular lines to form an X. Push a straight pin through the center of the circle. Hold the pin between your fingers. Rotate your circle to the different positions as shown. Observe what happens to the circle and the lines. As you move the circle, one line appears to shorten—this is the minor axis. The major axis is the long line; the minor axis is the short line. Take note that the minor axis line always lines up with the pin that you have put through the center of the circle.*

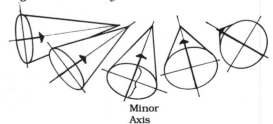

Minor Axis

☐ *Draw a page of squares in perspective and draw ellipses in them.*

Cylinders and Cones in Perspective

☐ *Draw a cylinder by first drawing a box in perspective. Then draw ellipses (circles in perspective) on opposite sides of the box. Connect these circles with straight lines to form a cylinder.*

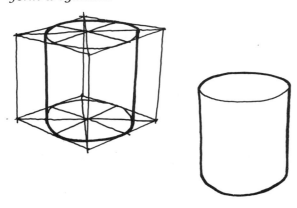

☐ *Draw a cone much the same way as a cylinder. But this time draw a circle on only one side of the box. On the opposite side of the box find the midpoint. Draw lines from the midpoint to edges of the circle. You have a cone.*

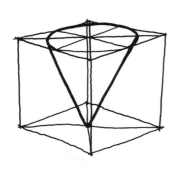

Your Goal

Eventually you should become so familiar with how circles appear when drawn in perspective that you can draw an accurate ellipse freehand. Use the square in perspective to aid you at first. Observe what happens to the circle with a pin through it. Soon you will become so familiar with ellipses that you will not need to draw the diagonals and midpoint lines through the square in order to accurately draw a circle in perspective.

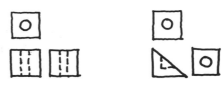

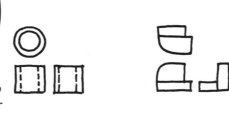

☐ *Remember before when you were to draw the three-dimensional view of an object after seeing the top view and two side views of the object? Do the same thing here that you did before. But this time the objects have circles or circular shapes in them. You will need to know how to draw ellipses in order to draw the right shape for the circle part of that object.*

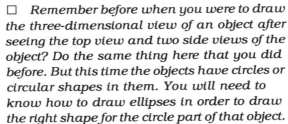

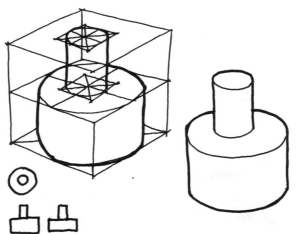

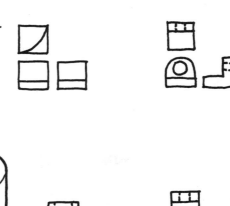

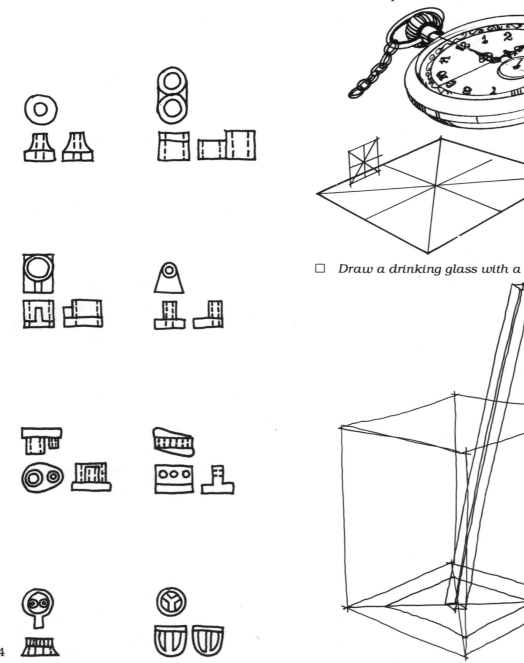

□ *Draw a pocketwatch.*

□ *Draw a wagon.*

□ *Draw a drinking glass with a straw in it.*

□ *Draw a planter.*

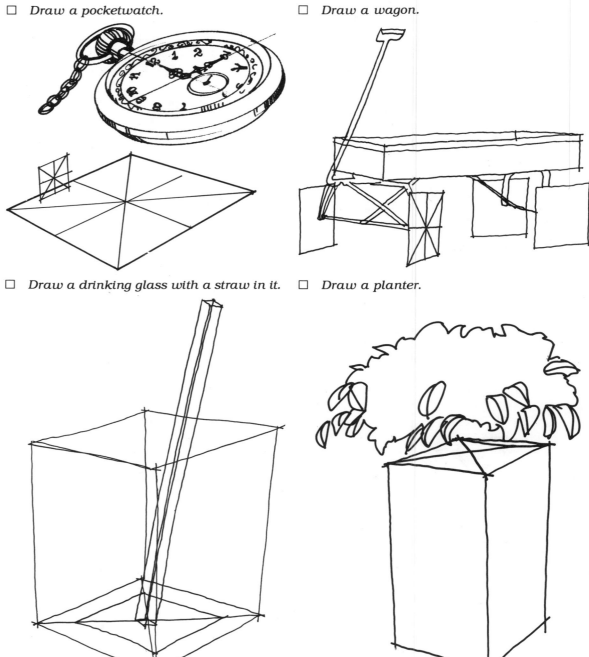

54

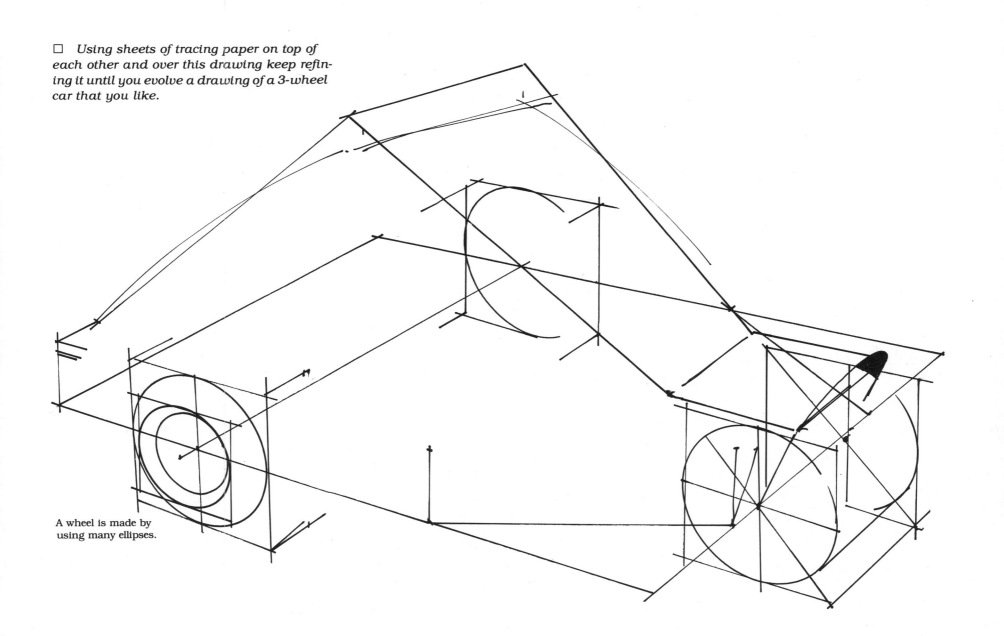

□ *Using sheets of tracing paper on top of each other and over this drawing keep refining it until you evolve a drawing of a 3-wheel car that you like.*

A wheel is made by using many ellipses.

The car on this page has many circular shapes. Most of these circular shapes will appear as ellipses because they will be circles drawn in perspective. The wheels and tires are examples.

55

Contour Lines

Contour lines are lines that wrap around objects showing what the surface of that object is like. They make two-dimensional flat objects appear to be solid, whole objects.

When it is without contour lines, the shape below looks like an oval. But, as you put the contour lines in, it gains the appearance of a third dimension so as to look like an egg. The jelly bean shape becomes three-dimensional because of the lines that wrap around it.

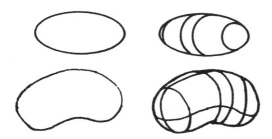

One Student's Experience with Contour Lines

I had one student whose ambition was to design automobiles. Before coming to my class, the automobiles that he would draw always came out wrong. When the class began drawing contour lines, he easily could understand why his automobiles appeared misshapen before. The contour lines around his cars gave that three-dimensional feeling that he needed in order to understand what was happening.

The same thing will happen for you. Contour lines around an object give a clear understanding of the third dimension of that portrayed object. No matter what the object—a car, a piece of furniture, a topographical map, or whatever—contour lines give a clear understanding of the dimension of the object. It is much easier to draw a three-dimensional object if you will see the object as though it had contour lines around it.

Feel The Surface

When drawing contour lines you should become conscious of your hand holding the pen and its pressure against the paper. Don't just draw the lines over the shape; feel the shape. Whether it is a car or a face, use your eye and hand to feel the contour line as it caresses the surface. Sense the contour as it travels down, around and into the picture exerting pressure on the paper as needed. With contour lines, more than any other technique, you must respond to that two-dimensional sketch as an actual three-dimensional object. Feel it!

□ *Draw the contour lines around the objects on this page. Feel the form as you draw it. Vary the pressure of your pen. Be sure to put a dark outer line—a cutting edge line—around each object.*

57

Contour Lines for Architecture

Architectural renderings of buildings and sites often use contour lines to help give a three-dimensional understanding to the building. You have probably seen models of proposed buildings where the ground is made by lying sheet upon sheet of cardboard to define the slope and incline of the terrain. These cardboard buildups are cut in varying sizes according to the contour map of the terrain.

The illustrations of the building here are enhanced by the contour lines. Without the lines the drawings would be rather dull and undescriptive. The contour lines help give form to the buildings.

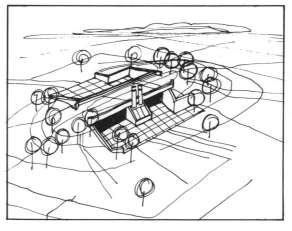

☐ *Try an exercise similar to the illustration shown here, using tree trunks. Draw the contour lines around tree trunks. Feel the surface as you do it. Know exactly where the bark goes in and out, where the knots are, where the imperfections in the wood occur. Those contour lines will help you understand the three-dimensional aspect of the wood.*

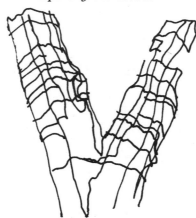

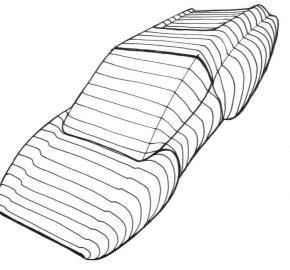

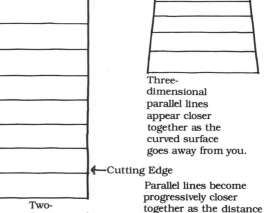

Three-dimensional parallel lines appear closer together as the curved surface goes away from you.

←Cutting Edge

Parallel lines become progressively closer together as the distance away from you increases.

Two-dimensional

☐ *The next exercise is to draw the contour lines around a speed shape. By speed shape I mean something like an automobile, or a rocket, or an airplane, or anything that moves fast.*

Contour Lines in Perspective

As parallel lines go away from you, they seem to get closer and closer. The ties on railroad tracks are an example of this visual phenomenon. The ties seem to get closer together as the tracks get farther from you. The illustration here demonstrates what happens to parallel lines when drawn in perspective. Also, lines that curve around a surface appear to get closer as the surface curves away from you.

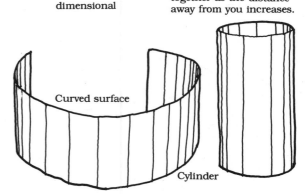

Curved surface

Cylinder

☐ *Draw equally distant lines on the objects below. Remember that even though the lines are equidistant they appear to get closer or farther apart as the surface weaves back and forth or goes into the distance.*

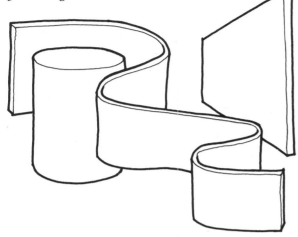

Changing Appearances with Contour Lines

Contour lines can change the entire appearance of an object. The car shown here is a new design from an existing automobile. The lines indicating the door lines, the molding down the side, and the fender shapes have been changed, thus changing the entire appearance of the car.

☐ *Put new contours over the automobiles shown here. Draw directly on the book. Copy the cars, but put on new contour lines to change the appearance of each car or truck.*

This is a photocopy of a car brochure—Try copying things you want to learn to draw at a light speed. Redraw the copies—changing and improving as you desire.

Shading

In life we see everything because a light source reflects off the surface. These reflections off objects are never pure, solid tones. We see every object as varying degrees of light or dark. This light and dark variation is called shading.

Shading gives form to objects. The basic shape objects shown here—a sphere, cylinder, cone, and cube—demonstrate different shading techniques. The top line is an example of no shading. The principle behind the shading process is quite simple: The closer to the direct light source, the lighter the tone of the object—the farther from the light source the darker the tone of the object.

Light   Light Gray   Dark Gray   Black

Many degrees of values can be seen on any object in real life. To make things more simple for rapid viz drawing, I suggest that you consider all objects as having only 4 degrees of value. From light to dark these values are: light, light gray, dark gray, and dark.

The cube demonstrates the four different degrees of value for shading. Speed is important when shading. Don't waste time trying to make things perfect. Move from dark to light quickly using only the four values listed above.

Remember that the direction of the light determines the value of the shading on the surface.

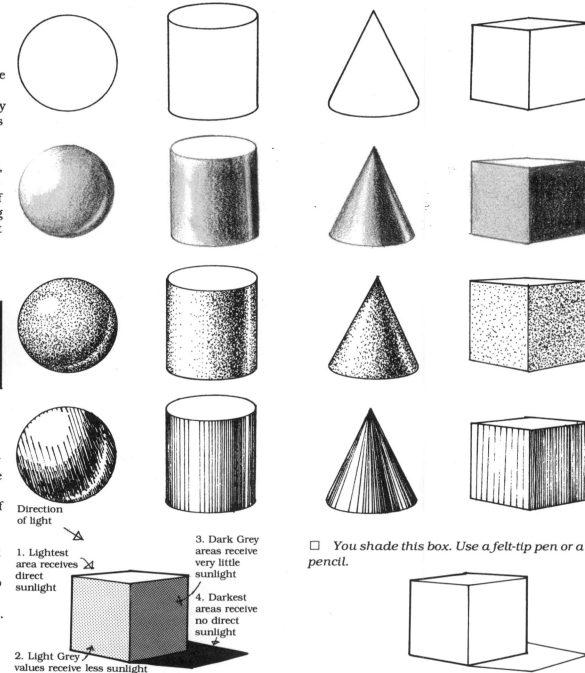

Direction of light

1. Lightest area receives direct sunlight

2. Light Grey values receive less sunlight

3. Dark Grey areas receive very little sunlight

4. Darkest areas receive no direct sunlight

☐ *You shade this box. Use a felt-tip pen or a pencil.*

☐ *Use a pencil or a felt tip pen to indicate the shading on the object shown here. The areas have been marked as to what value they should be (1 is lightest and 4 is darkest).*

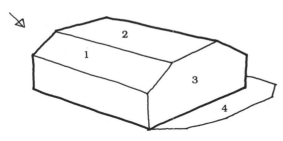

☐ *The light source is indicated. You put the correct shading on the objects below.*

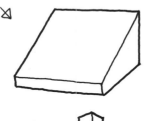

Direction of light

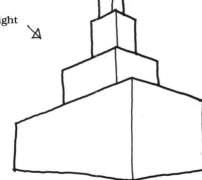

Direction of light

Test Your Materials

Before shading anything you ought to experiment with your drawing tool (pen or pencil) and the drawing surface. Especially be careful with felt-tip pens. Some papers soak up the ink while others don't. What looks gray on one drawing surface is jet black on another. Experiment before you begin drawing—get the feel of the tool and the paper.

Shading Curved Surfaces

Shading a curved surface is very much like shading a plane surface. The only difference is that the shading gradually changes from light to dark. Curved surfaces do not have a distinct edge to separate the value tones of the shading. Gradually blend the white to gray to black shading on a curved surface. This rule applies to all curved surfaces—a pipe, a cylinder, an arm, and so on.

Direction of light

Light gradually curves around a curved surface.

☐ *Shade the curved surfaces shown here. Always remember that the light source dictates how things should be shaded.*

Direction of light

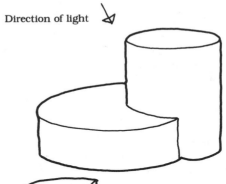

Direction of light

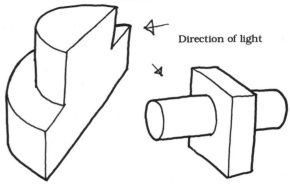

Direction of light

Direction of light

Reflected Light

If you look closely at objects you will notice that reflected light is nearly always visible. The most noticeable place is on curved surfaces like a sphere or a cylinder. Near the darkest part (core) of the object there is usually an area of light. Study the examples here to see how to draw this core area of reflected light.

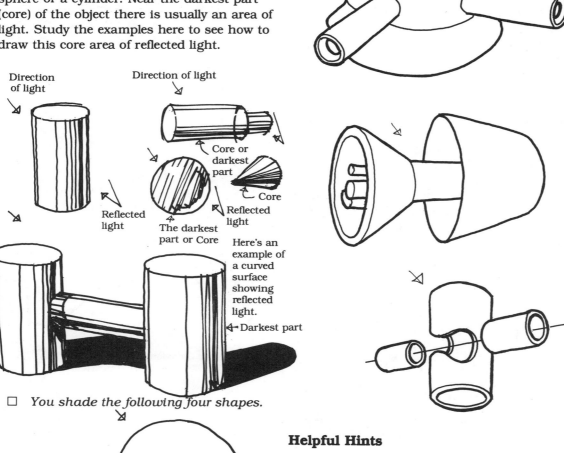

Direction of light

Direction of light

Core or darkest part

Core

Reflected light

Reflected light

The darkest part or Core

Here's an example of a curved surface showing reflected light.

← Darkest part

☐ *You shade the following four shapes.*

cept seems to confuse many students. Look at the cylinders. The one on the left is the same as the one on the right except that it has more lines to indicate the shading. These extra lines make the left cylinder appear to be a darker color cylinder than the one on the right.

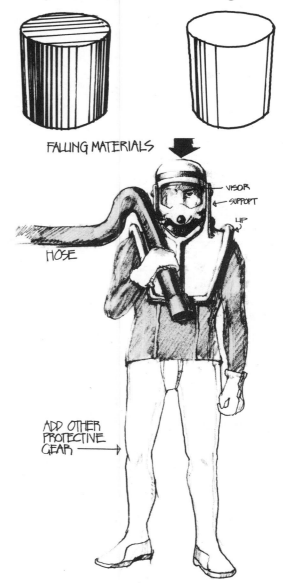

FALLING MATERIALS

VISOR

SUPPORT

LIP

HOSE

ADD OTHER PROTECTIVE GEAR →

Helpful Hints

This page and the next page contain hints that can help you in your attempt to master shading and shadows. I try to do three things in all my drawings: 1) the darker the object is the darker the shading, 2) light goes against dark, and 3) always put subtle line variations even on plain flat surfaces.

"The darker the object, the darker the shading" sounds simple enough, but the con-

□ *Shade the following objects.*

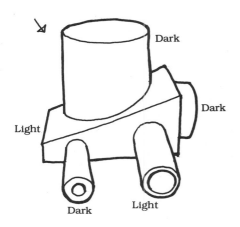

Dark

Dark

Light

Dark   Light

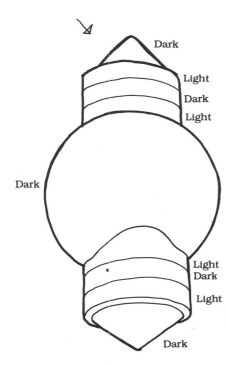

Dark

Light

Dark

Light

Dark

Light
Dark

Light

Dark

Remember the core on curved surfaces.

Light Against Dark

Good drawing uses the principle of continuous light against dark. The trees below demonstrate this phenomenon. The trunk of the tree goes from dark to light and back to dark again. Where the tree trunk crosses a light background the trunk appears to be dark. Where the tree trunk crosses a dark background it appears to be light. Make this very obvious in your drawings—put dark against light. Begin by drawing the dark in first then proceed to the lighter shades.

□ *Copy the picture of the trees. Do your drawing in the box below.*

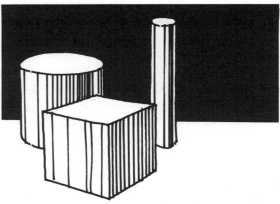

The strongest point of emphasis is where the darkest dark or the lightest light contrasts with the surroundings. If you can play the darkest dark against the lightest light then you have the strongest point of contrast in the drawing. This high contrast area demands the most attention from the viewer.

Add subtle line variations to flat surfaces to make them appear more realistic.

Subtle Variations

Things seldom if ever appear to be flat, smooth surfaces without degrees of shading in real life. There is always a degree of variation in shading on all objects. Study smooth surfaces of things around you to see how reflections, shading, shadows, dirt, and other imperfections make those surfaces appear to have light and dark areas. You can indicate these subtle variations in your drawings by adding a few scribbly lines. Remember that in real life there is always a subtle variation in shading even on the most flat surfaces.

□ *Below is a car to practice shading on. Some of the drawing has been completed to give you an idea of how the shading is done. You finish the drawing.*

□ *After finishing the car, redraw the other objects on this page. Do each object larger than shown here. Put in the correct shading.*

Shade Basic Shapes

When learning to do shading many people get confused as the objects appear more complex. If you will learn to see each object as being composed of many simple basic shapes, you will have an easier time shading those objects. Take the radio shown here; the radio is a basic box shape, the knobs are small cylinders, and so on. Shade each basic shape individually and when finished the whole will be shaded correctly.

If you have problems with these concepts try getting some objects that are just basic shapes. Take them into a dark room and turn on a single light source. You will see in real life the same things I'm talking about in this book.

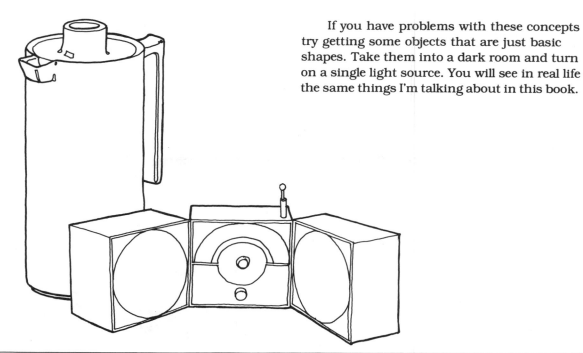

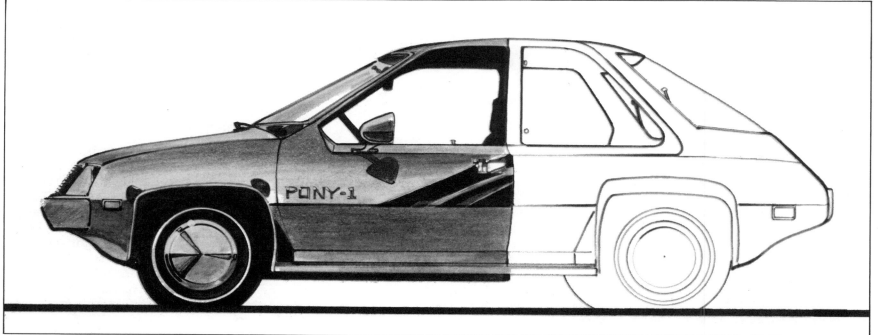

Color

This book deals with black and white drawing. We have not even touched upon color. The book is not printed in color and so it is impossible to really tell what happens with color. Color is a new subject all its own. It is very technical and there are many things to know in order to handle color well.

Let me just say that for most drawings, architectural drawings or product drawings, it is best to use color sparingly. Use it to emphasize points or to give a little more feeling to the drawing.

Principles Governing Color

1. For rapid viz type drawings, use color sparingly. In the kinds of drawings discussed in this book you should use two or three levels of color at the most. Your dominant color should be your brightest—the color that would demand the most attention. Your subordinate color should be complementary, but it should be very much less demanding. Your third color would be considerably more subdued and should demand very little attention at all.

2. Use complementary colors. If the colors you choose contrast rather than complement each other, then the viewer will be more attracted to the fight between the colors than to the colors and drawing.

3. Light colors advance—they punch out. Dark colors recede—they appear to be holes or to go back in.

4. Most shadows in objects are drawn kind of bluish in color because they reflect the sky.

5. The paper affects the appearance of color. Always test your drawing tool (pen, magic marker, brush, etc.) on the paper you intend to use to see what the color will be.

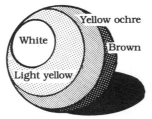

If you were to make this ball yellow, these are the colors you would probably use to show the shading, the highlights, and to make the ball look real.

Draw What You See

One very common error when drawing in color is to draw what you think you see rather than what you see. Colored objects usually have a variety of colors, yet people draw them as one color. Reflected color and shadows change the color of the object. Even though a wall has been painted yellow in reality, it appears to be yellow, brown, blue, black, and so on because of shadows and reflected light from surrounding objects. You must draw the wall with many colors to make it more realistic. Draw what you actually see, not what you think you should see.

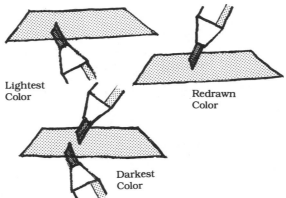

Lightest Color

Redrawn Color

Darkest Color

One Color Makes Many

Rapid viz drawing, as explained in the drawing process section, employs tracing the original sketch until it is as you want it for the end result. Since you are working with a somewhat transparent paper, you can use the transparency to help give you more color. The same color applied to different sides of the paper appears to be different values of color (see drawing).

Final Word of Caution

Color is like dynamite. It should be used cautiously. It should be used just in the right spot to put in a little bit of emphasis. Too much color can ruin a drawing.

☐ *Color the following shapes:*
a box, a sphere, a cone, and a cylinder.

☐ *Color the following shapes made on these combinations:*
a cone, two cylinders, and a cube;
two cubes and a sphere;
a cylinder, a sphere, and a cube.

Don't draw everything in the drawing. Be selective.

Shadows

Drawing cast shadows is difficult for most people as they begin to draw. But shadows shouldn't be difficult. The principle of shadows is really very simple. A shadow is the base of a triangle formed by the direction of the light source and the object.

☐ *Study the visual explanation of how to draw shadows on this page.*

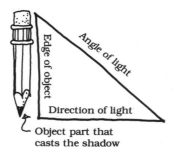

Angle and Direction of light when put next to the edge or side of the object form a triangle. This triangle helps you determine the cast shadow.

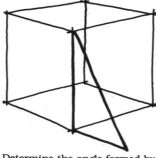

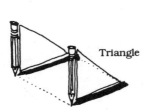

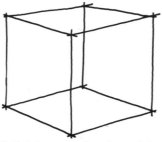

Let's take a simple cube and draw the cast shadow.

Think of the cube as being transparent so that you can see the hidden sides and edges of the cube.

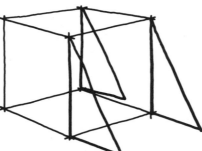

Determine the angle formed by the light source and the cube side.

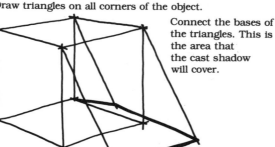

Draw triangles on all corners of the object.

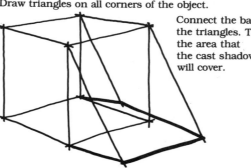

Connect the bases of the triangles. This is the area that the cast shadow will cover.

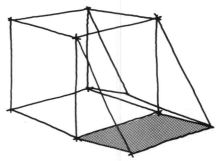

Darken in the cast shadow area.

Steps to Draw Cast Shadows

1. Determine the angle of the light source.
2. Draw the triangle on all edges of the object.
3. Connect the bases of the triangles.
4. Darken in the cast shadow area.

☐ *Draw the cast shadow on the cube below. The only thing different from the cubes above is that the light source is from a different direction. Determine the light direction yourself.*

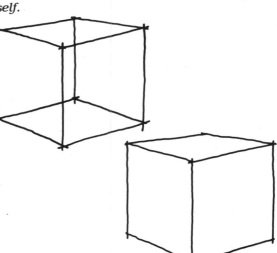

Shadows for Complicated Objects

The cast shadow of complicated objects is drawn the same as for simple objects. You first draw the triangle formed by the object and the light source. Base of the triangle is the cast shadow.

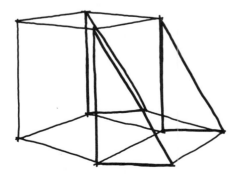

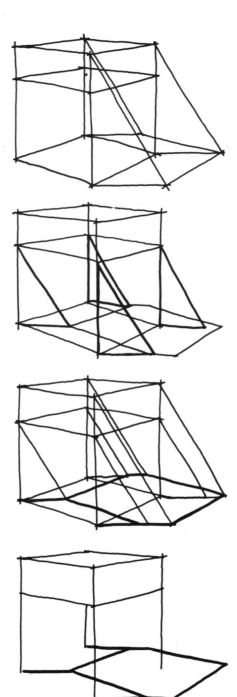

☐ *Study the steps for drawing the cast shadow of this table. Then you try drawing the shadow for the table. Copy exactly what I have done here. Draw the cast shadow lightly first, then darken it in later.*

Shadows Over Objects

The shadow that falls over another object is drawn the same way as over a flat surface. Study the example here.

Notice how the cast shadow appears to be shorter where it crosses the smaller cube. This happens because the triangle crosses the cube higher up so that the base of the triangle is shorter.

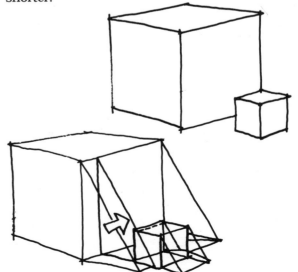

67

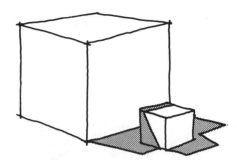

A shadow that falls over a hole is done the same way. But notice that the shadow is longer because of the extra distance from the ground surface to the bottom of the hole.

Shadows for Curved Surfaces

Shadows from curved surfaces are done the same as for flat surfaces. The light source forms a triangle. You run this imaginary triangle along the curved surface to plot the area of the cast shadow.

A cast shadow that falls over a curved surface is determined the same way, by finding the triangle and repeating it along the shadow casting surface.

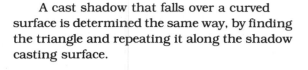

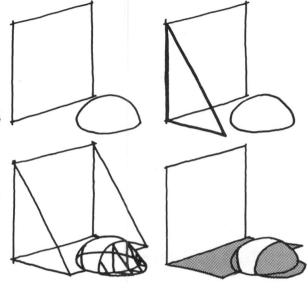

Complicated Cast Shadows

Let's review again the process for determining cast shadows. It is the same process no matter how complicated the shadow appears.

1. Determine the angle of the light source.
2. Imagine the object as being transparent so that you can see all the sides and edges.
3. Draw the angle from all major edges and corners.
4. Connect the bases of the triangles to determine the cast shadow.
5. Remove the lines for the triangles and the transparent lines of the object.
6. Darken the cast shadow area.

You Try It

Many different objects are shown here. The cast shadow for the many different objects will appear quite different although they are all drawn using the same formula.

☐ *Draw the cast shadow for these objects. Remember to draw the transparent edges to help you find the cast shadows. Also, watch the direction of the light source.*

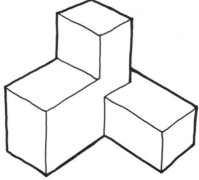

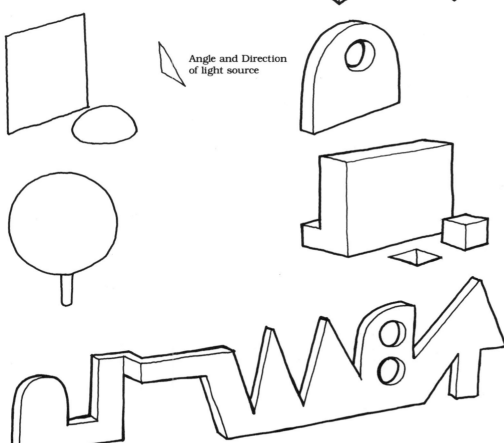

Angle and Direction of light source

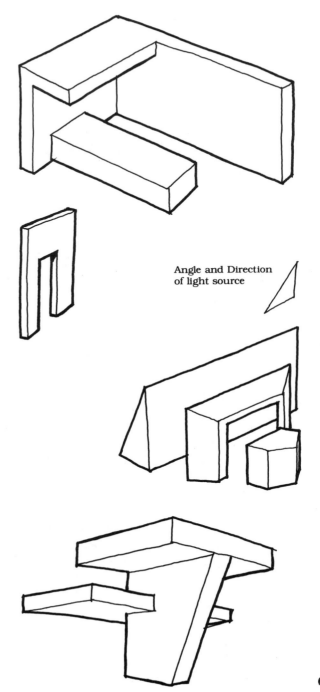

Angle and Direction of light source

☐ *The angle and direction of the light are indicated for each object. Draw the correct cast shadow.*

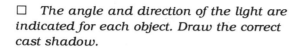

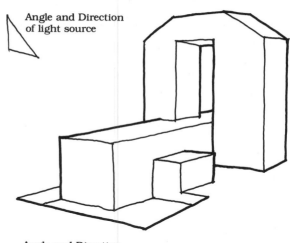

Angle and Direction of light source

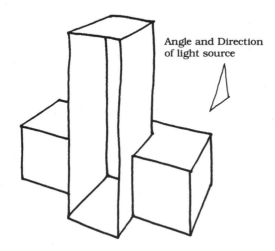

Angle and Direction of light source

Angle and Direction of light source

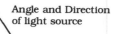

Angle and Direction of light source

Angle and Direction of light source

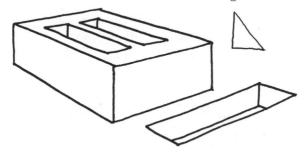

Don't let this complicated shape confuse you. Refer back to the basic shading and shadow principles. Treat the object as many simple basic shapes combined to form one more complex object.

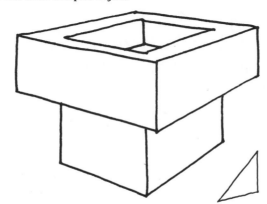

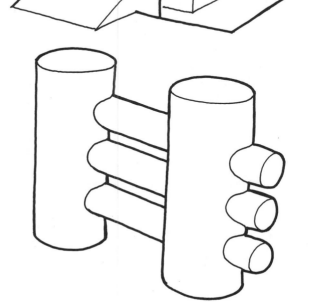

□ *Add shading, shadows, and other details to make this drawing more interesting.*

Rapid Viz Shadows and Shading

These two pages contain examples of quick sketch drawings by professionals who use rapid viz techniques. The drawings have been done by architects, interior designers, product designers, and landscape architects. As you study the drawings, especially take note of the following points:

1. The contrast of very light against very dark is used to emphasize.
2. Sometimes the various tones or values are indicated by quick loose lines—scribbly lines—to make the surfaces appear more realistic.
3. Cast shadows greatly enhance a drawing.
4. Sometimes drawings are seen totally as degrees of shadow and shading with very little detail other than light and dark shading.

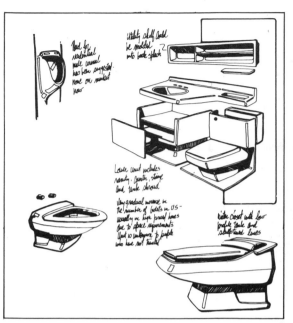

7 8

9

8

10

11

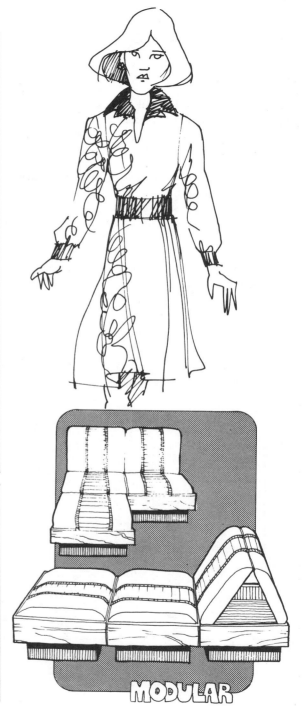

MODULAR

Reflections

You will find it very helpful to learn to draw reflections of different objects. If buildings sit near water, for example, there is a reflection in the water of buildings. Many home and office products have chrome or shiny surfaces that show reflections. Glass windows and mirrors are other reflective surfaces that will often appear in your drawings. If you can indicate the reflection, it lends a great deal of reality to any drawing.

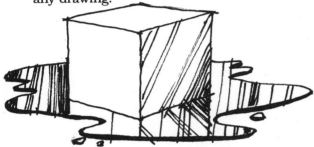

A reflection is very simple to draw. It is a mirror image of the object.

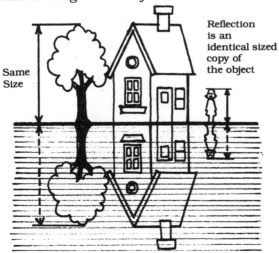

Same Size

Reflection is an identical sized copy of the object

Notice the house and the tree with the girl standing by. The exact mirror image drawn below it is the reflection.

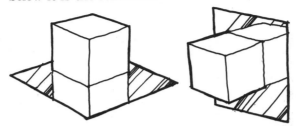

Drawing reflections consists primarily of drawing the object first and then plotting the reflection. Measurements on the reflection are the same as those on the object. If an object is sitting exactly on the ground or exactly on the surface of the water, the reflection begins at the baseline and is a mirror image.

Equal distance from object to reflective surface and reflective surface to reflected image

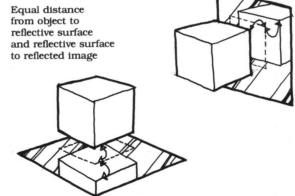

If your object sits above the reflecting surface, then you must take into account the distance from the base of the object to the reflecting surface. Measure the distance from the object to the reflecting surface. Then measure that same distance beneath the reflecting surface. See the example.

Sometimes a nonreflecting surface interferes with the reflection. In this case draw the reflection as if it were all reflecting and then erase the part within the non-reflecting area.

Reflected image on water is not as clear and complete as original object.

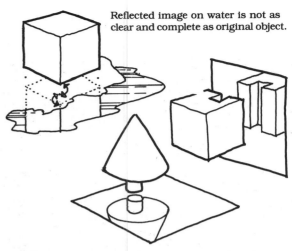

A reflection can show parts of the object that you would not see without the reflection. If you are above an object, and if that same object is above water, you will see the top of the object while the reflection will show the bottom of the object.

☐ *Shown here are reflections on glass, reflections on water, and so on. As you see, some of the reflections are started, but not finished. You complete the reflections so that you will get an idea of how it is done.*

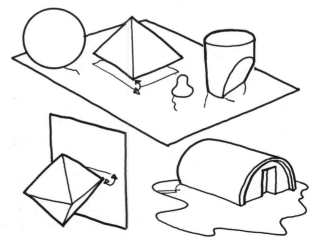

Complicated Reflections

Drawing reflections is very simple. Don't let complex drawings frighten you. The reflection is just a mirror image of the original object. Take it a small part at a time until you complete the whole.

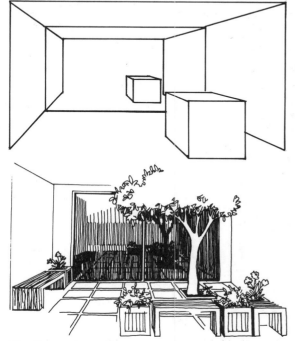

☐ *Copy the reflection in the glass surface below just as it is done above.*

☐ *Do the water reflection the same as shown above.*

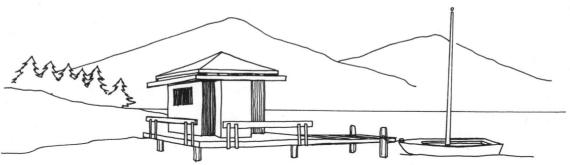

Summary

Listed here are the general principles to remember when drawing reflections.

1. The reflected image is a mirror image.
2. Draw the reflected image in perspective the same as the original.
3. The reflected image is not as clear as the original.
4. Things not seen on the original are sometimes seen on the reflection.
5. The reflected image is the same distance from the reflective surface as is the original from the reflective surface.

☐ *Finish drawing this half-finished waterfront scene. Include reflections and other details (windows on buildings, more buildings, people, etc.)*

☐ *Draw the reflection in the store window above.*

When a shadow falls across the window, you see inside the building rather than seeing the reflection on the window.

☐ *Illustrate three bathroom fixtures. Remember that the chrome on the fixtures will reflect images of other objects in the bathroom.*

☐ *Go through a home decorating magazine, or a design magazine and collect at least 10 examples of photos or illustrations that show reflections. This should be the beginning of your scrap file of reflected images. An extensive file will be necessary if you are to become proficient at drawing reflections.*

Rapid Indication

What is rapid indication and why is it important? Well, many drawings require subordinate elements that need to be there in order to set up what is happening. These other elements, other objects, are not important except that they set up an environment in which you can view the most important element in the drawing. The secondary parts of the drawing need not be very complex, exact, or detailed, but need to be there so that the total drawing can be understood. They may be people, plants, hands, automobiles, mountains, or just about anything that can be used to complement the key elements in your drawings.

Let me give you an example. I had one student in a class who, right before your eyes, could quickly make a drawing with all of the elements in place. The rest of the students in the class were quite astounded that he could so quickly and so easily put total drawings together. It took the other students awhile to understand what was happening, but they finally caught on. What he was doing was quickly drawing some elements and other elements he was making more detailed. He had visually memorized the secondary elements that were needed for most drawings, making it easy for him to draw their respective forms. This left him time to concentrate on the more important parts of his drawing.

Rapid indication, then, is learning to draw the sketchy subordinate elements in the drawing, and learning to draw those elements quickly and easily. The subordinate elements must help to emphasize the main object in the drawing—they should not detract from or compete with the main object.

Mental Rubber Stamps

Think of indicated objects in a drawing as rubber stamp images. It is as though you become so familiar with certain things that you draw them almost as quickly as you could rubber stamp them. As if rubber stamped, the objects you draw look almost identical. The

There are many ways to indicate a figure. You choose the method that best fits and complements your drawing.

78

drawing process becomes so automatic for drawing the subordinate objects that you have more time to concentrate on making the important parts of your drawing better.

The Completed Picture

Why do you need these subordinate indicated elements? Most main elements in a drawing—buildings or products that you are drawing—are usually seen in their final context. If it is a building, for example, it will have trees around it and people going into the building after the building is built. If it is a product, it will be seen in a room or in an office or on the shelves of a store. You need to learn how to draw these surroundings in which the final product will be seen. By including the natural surroundings in your drawings you give a greater visual understanding of the actual object that you are showing.

Once again, the things that we are talking about *indicating* are subordinate objects in a drawing. They are never primary objects; they are always subordinate.

One of the steps in learning how to do rapid indication is to first determine what is most important in the drawing. Is it the building? If it is, then don't draw the building too

sketchy and loose. Draw it more detailed and draw the surroundings very sketchy and loose. Don't put so much detail in the people and in the foliage surrounding the building that you lose sight of the building. It is important to have the building be your most detailed and most accurate item in the drawing. Have the people and the foliage be very sketchy and very loose.

I want to show you how to draw the sketchy, loose surroundings. Remember, using these surrounding elements will create involvement between the viewer and the drawing. If you can put people in a drawing, the drawing seems more real, more inviting.

An Inflated Example

Shown across the bottom of these two pages is an inflatable chair. We have indicated an individual sitting in that chair. The most important element is the chair. Therefore, all of the drawings of individuals should be subordinate to the chair. There are, as you can see, many different ways of indicating the person sitting in the chair. They all work well if used in the correct setting. You need to be the one to determine how detailed you want to draw the person sitting in the chair.

Be careful not to allow your indication to overpower the main element in the drawing. The girl here overpowers the chair, yet the chair should be the main element.

The drawing of the woman playing the guitar in the last chair is an exception. This figure is overdone. A major tendency of beginners is to overdo indicated figures. Beware not to do it. An indication is just that—it is an *indication* of an object. It is not a detailed rendering. You are emphasizing the chair. Don't overdo the rapid indication.

Key Points of Rapid Indication

1. Keep indicated objects simple. Emphasize the critical points necessary to communicate the main element in the drawing. All other surrounding elements can be simplified even to the point of mere outline or silhouette in some drawings.
2. Subordinate all indicated objects. Put your emphasis on the major things you are trying to communicate. Have things such as plants, people, hands, buildings, and the like compliment the main element in the drawing.
3. Economize on indicated objects. Do indicated objects by using the fewest lines, shapes, and parts necessary. Spend your time on the important dominant elements in the drawing. Make the indicated parts as quickly as possible.

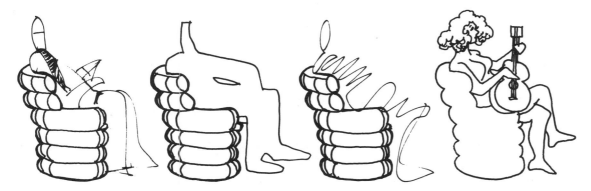

79

Figure Indication

Bear in mind that most objects you will be drawing are going to be ridden in, sat upon, looked at, talked into, activated, operated, or in some other way used by people.

The drawings shown on the right look austere and empty because there are no people shown. They are drawings showing human environments and so people are critical to the visual description shown.

Most beginners have the tendency to over-draw the figure making it look awkward. The figures shown below are typical examples of the kind often used by designers and architects.

☐ *Draw 5 more figures in the style started on each line.*

☐ *On tracing paper, quickly redraw the two environments shown on this page but include figures of people. Try different arrangements and styles until you feel that your solution looks good.*

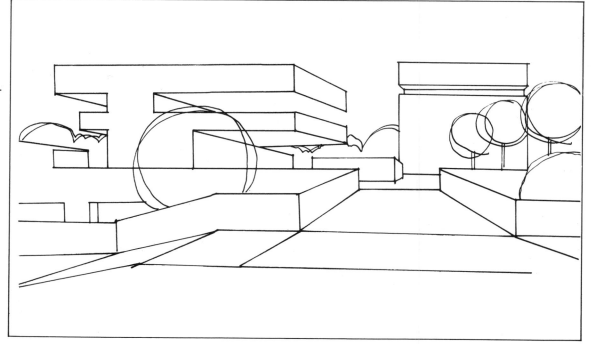

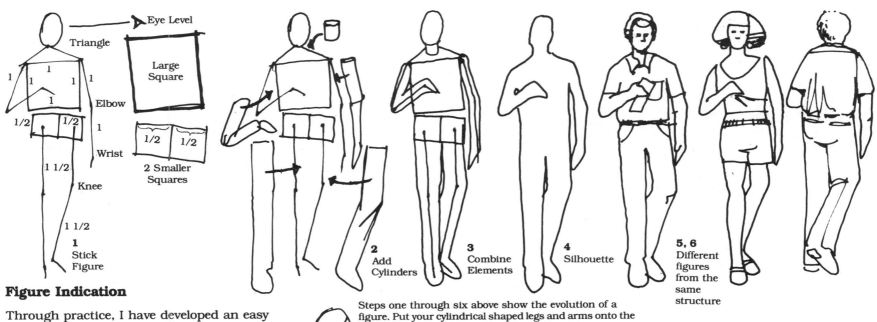

1
Stick
Figure

Eye Level

Triangle

Large Square

Elbow

Wrist

Knee

1 1/2

1 1/2

2 Smaller Squares

2
Add Cylinders

3
Combine Elements

4
Silhouette

5, 6
Different figures from the same structure

Figure Indication

Through practice, I have developed an easy method to quickly draw a person. First draw a square. This square is the torso of the person. On top of this square draw a flattened triangle with an oval above it. Below the square draw two more squares that are equal in size. The sides of the smaller squares are about one-half the length of the side of the larger square. The length from the shoulder to the elbow and the elbow to the wrist is equal to a side of the larger square. The length of the thigh to the knee and the knee to the ankle is one and one-half the length of a side of the large square.

The female figure is more rounded, has smaller chest and larger hips.

The male figure is more angular, has a larger chest and smaller hips.

Steps one through six above show the evolution of a figure. Put your cylindrical shaped legs and arms onto the basic figure. Make the outer shape define the figure—add detail to finish the figure as you desire.

Remember the figure has depth.

Tilt the boxes at different angles. That is the way people stand. Rather than being stiff and straight, people stand at an angle, leaning, or with weight shifted to one leg.

When drawing people in a finished drawing draw groups of people—an odd number of people in the group is better. A single person in a drawing attracts attention. You want the figure to compliment the main element in the drawing, not to attract attention.

Tilt the figure for more realism.

81

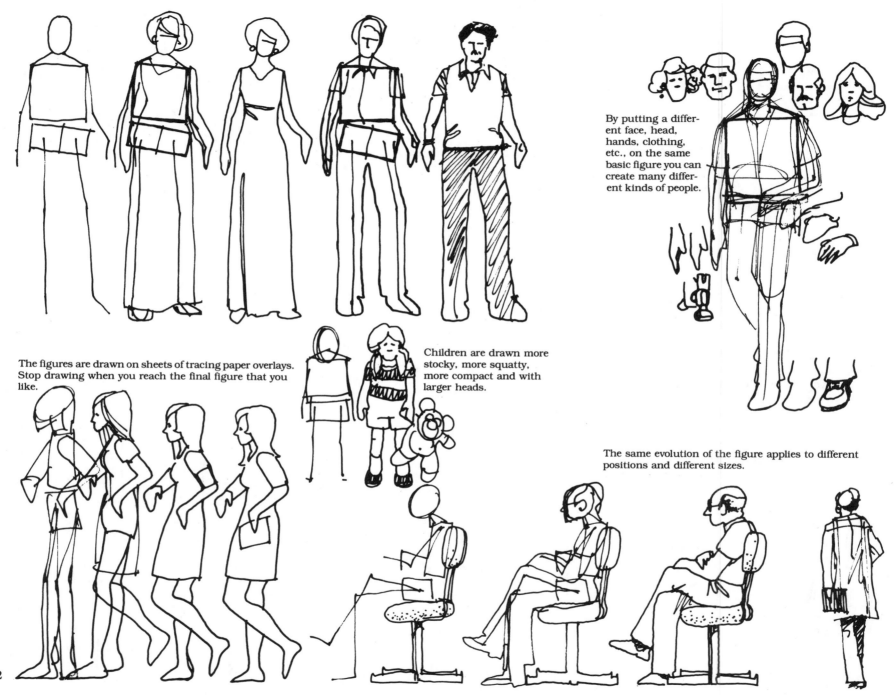

By putting a different face, head, hands, clothing, etc., on the same basic figure you can create many different kinds of people.

The figures are drawn on sheets of tracing paper overlays. Stop drawing when you reach the final figure that you like.

Children are drawn more stocky, more squatty, more compact and with larger heads.

The same evolution of the figure applies to different positions and different sizes.

82

Figure Exercises

☐ *Many figures are started below. Lay a piece of tracing paper over the ones shown and evolve these figures into the kind of person that you want. Make up any kind of person. It often takes two or more paper overlays to get the figure the way you want it.*

83

Figures Establish Scale

Human figures establish scale in drawings. A person next to an object in a drawing tells the viewer the size of the object.

☐   *Use this page to draw people next to pens of varying size scales similar to the way it is done in the drawings below.*

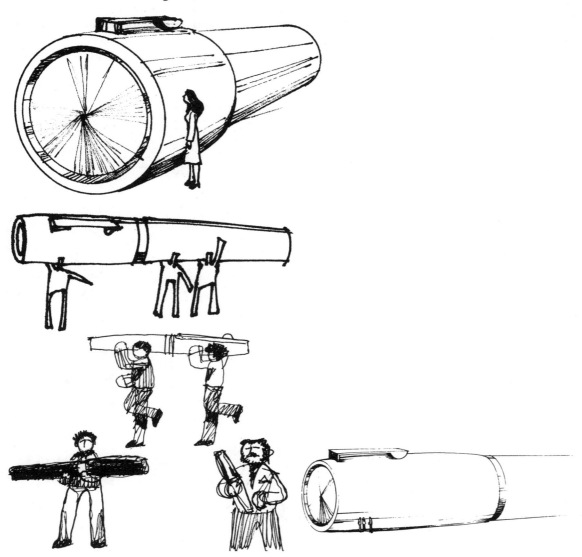

People in Drawings

The different drawings on this page contain indicated people. As you can see, the people shown are very simple and are done in many different drawing styles. There is no one set kind of figure indication that will work for all drawings. The process used to draw the figures is similar for all the drawings, but the detail varies. Thus, the people appear different in each example. The purpose of your drawing, your abilities, your time, and your interests will determine the kind of indicated figures you draw.

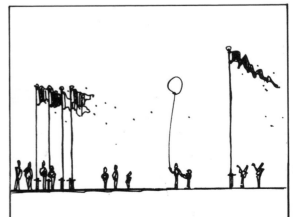

Hands

Human hands are one of the most difficult parts of the body to draw correctly. It is tedious, difficult, and time consuming to carefully draw a hand as it really looks,. But to rapidly indicate hands is not difficult. Three "tricks" will help you draw hands:

1. Don't draw everything. Just the outer edge and a few key lines make a hand. Details must be drawn correctly if they are included. Only draw the essential lines and no more. You can stylize the hand to further simplify the hand.
2. What the hand does is the reason for the hand. Keep the emphasis on the actions the hand is doing.
3. Draw from life. Make Polaroids or have someone pose in the position you want to draw. If you don't draw from life, chances

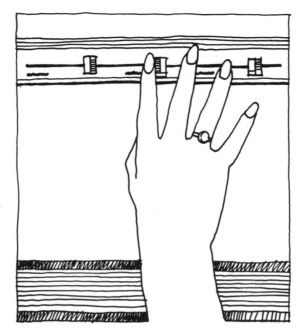

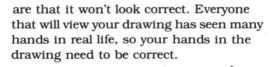

☐ *Draw two hands holding a rod.*

are that it won't look correct. Everyone that will view your drawing has seen many hands in real life, so your hands in the drawing need to be correct.

☐ *Draw a hand using the bottom clippers. Use tracing paper if needed.*

☐ *Draw a hand pushing a button.*

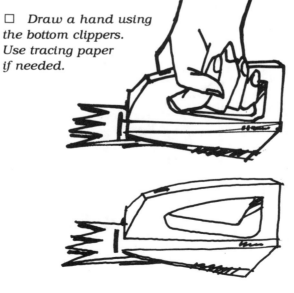

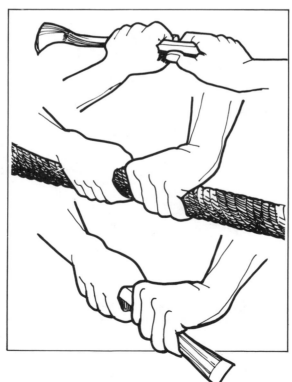

86

Insert People

This drawing lacks pizzaz. The absence of people makes everything look sterile and uninviting. The indicated presence of people in drawings makes the drawings more inviting.

☐ *Lay a piece of tracing paper over the drawing. Redraw it with people indicated. Be sure to stylize and simplify the people so that the people do not demand too much viewer attention—the building is the main element in the drawing. The drawing might also need other indicated objects such as cars or foliage. You decide.*

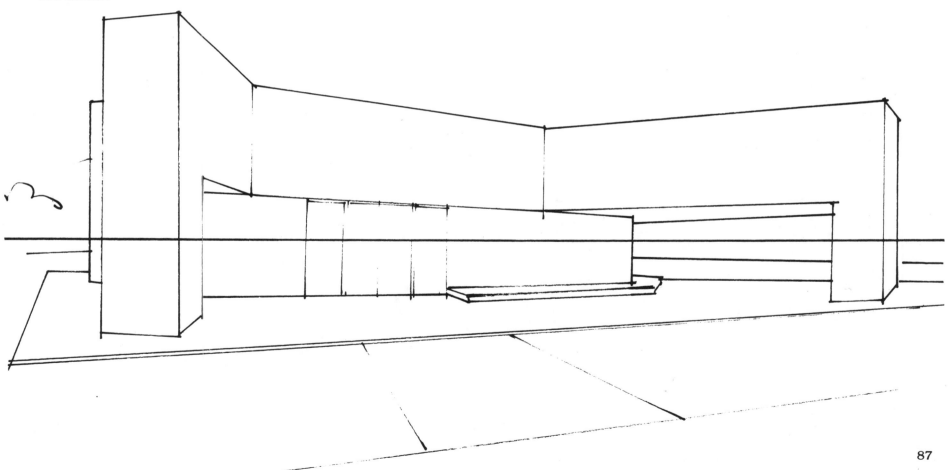

Arrows

You will find that knowing how to draw interesting arrows can aid you in drawings that communicate concepts, i.e., designing buildings or products. Learn how to draw a great many arrows. Draw arrows with curves in them, three-dimensional arrows, arrows in groups, large arrows, fat arrows, small arrows, wavy arrows. Draw arrows that turn, arrows that spin, arrows that come out of boxes at different angles. Try drawing positive arrows, (black arrows on white background), negative arrows (white arrow against dark background), dark arrows, or light arrows.

You will find that just knowing how to draw different kinds of arrows can help you explain points in your drawing and visually enhance your drawings.

I once had a psychologist tell me that people who like to draw arrows are very achievement oriented. They like to go after goals. If that is true you might want to put yourself more on the road to success by drawing more arrows and becoming more goal oriented. I think the real reason designers like them is that they look neat.

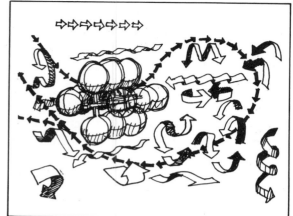

88

□ *Fill this page with different kinds of arrows.*

Indicating Plants

Another drawing skill you'll find helpful is knowing how to quickly draw plants and foliage. The key to drawing plants is to know the basic shape of the plant and then to use the different line techniques shown to complete the plant.

By applying these line techniques to this basic branch structure you can make many different kinds of plants.

The basic shape of the trees shown is a circle. The different kinds of trees are illustrated by the different line techniques.

Indoor plants are created the same as all other foliage. First learn the shape of the plant, then use various line techniques to indicate different plant varieties.

Ground cover is drawn by using different kinds of line. The lines indicate varying textures, but detail is left to the viewer to imagine.

The drawings on this page evolve through different stages. The same basic kind of tree or plant is shown in varying degrees of abstraction and detail or lack of detail.

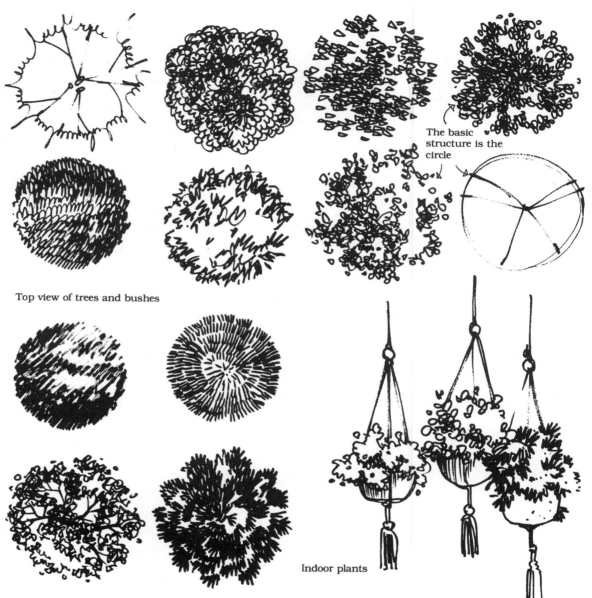

The basic structure is the circle

Top view of trees and bushes

Indoor plants

Ground cover

Deciduous Trees

Coniferous Trees

Plants in containers

Bushes

91

Examples of Plants

The secret to rapidly drawing plants and foliage is to draw the "feel" of the plants and not the detail. Use the line technique to give feeling you'd expect from the situation. Study the examples on this page to understand the concept of feeling rather than detail.

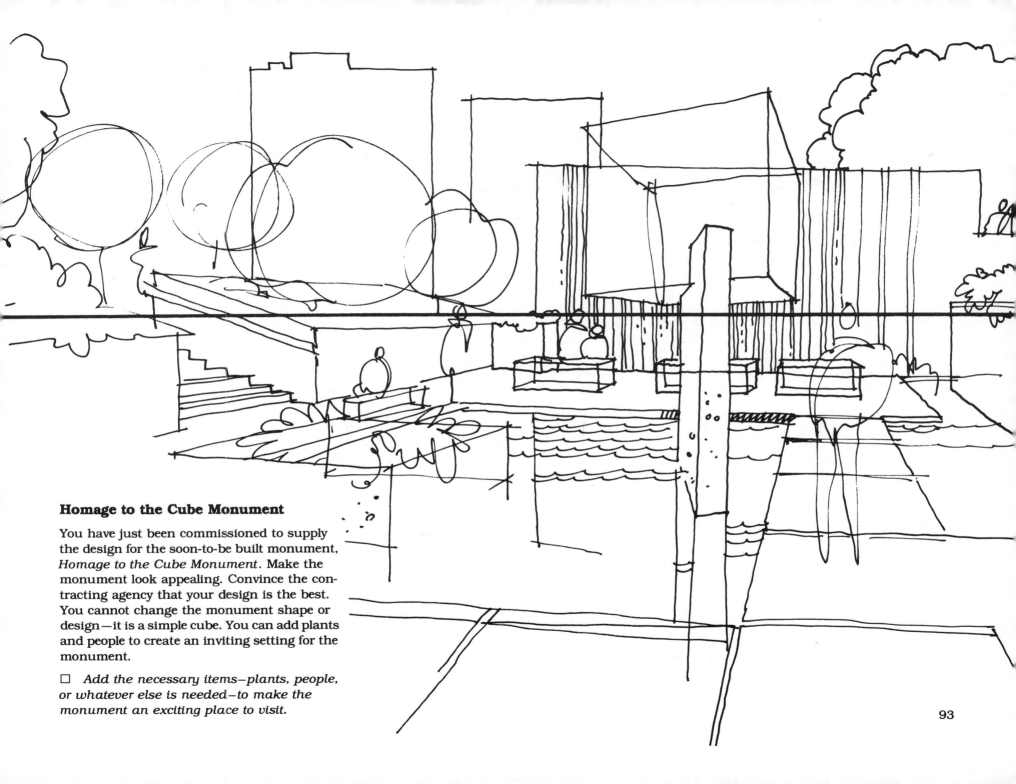

Homage to the Cube Monument

You have just been commissioned to supply the design for the soon-to-be built monument, *Homage to the Cube Monument*. Make the monument look appealing. Convince the contracting agency that your design is the best. You cannot change the monument shape or design—it is a simple cube. You can add plants and people to create an inviting setting for the monument.

☐ *Add the necessary items—plants, people, or whatever else is needed—to make the monument an exciting place to visit.*

93

The Clinic Waiting Room

☐ *This rough drawing is a clinic waiting room (such as a doctor's office). Use your design talents to make the drawing look inviting. Use tracing paper overlays to finish the drawing. Add rapidly indicated elements that will enhance the drawing.*

94

Lettering

Another skill that you will find helpful for good drawing is learning how to rapidly draw letterforms. You will want to know how to indicate different styles of alphabets and letterforms. Once you learn how alphabet styles differ you can quickly indicate a kind of lettering by imitating the basic design of that letterform.

So that you might get a basic understanding of alphabets and letterforms, I suggest buying a book or two and tracing some of the different alphabets.

A good book is *The Type Specimen Book,* published by Van Nostrand Reinhold (in paperback). Another source of letterforms is to request catalogs from rub-on lettering companies. These catalogs contain an excellent variety of different alphabets.

As you do drawings, you might find it helpful to put refined lettering on your drawing by using rub-on letters.

Below are two alphabets that were drawn by placing tracing paper over printed alphabets in type specimen books. By using this same technique you can add finished lettering to your drawing where applicable to improve the drawing.

Many Kinds of Lettering from One

On the next page is an example of one person's lettering of several alphabets. By changing the size of the letters, the height of the lower case letters, the line thickness and so on, one person can create many different styles of letters.

The secret to drawing good alphabets is consistency. The vertical and horizontal lines should be parallel. The first alphabet lacks this quality. It is not consistent; lines are not parallel and the slant of the letters is not uniform.

ABCDEFGHIJKLMNOPQRS
TUVWXYZ!?,
1234567890 $¢ %+

By tracing alphabets from type specimen books, you can add a finished look to your drawings.

ABCDEFGHIJKLMN
OPQRSTUVWXYZ
1234567890 &

ABCDEFGHIJKLMNOPQRSTUVW /I\I\I E
XYZ 1234567890

ABCDEFGHIJKLMNOPQRSTUVW E≡
XYZ 1234567890

ABCDEFGHIJKLMNOPQRSTUVWXYZ E≡
1234567890

ABCDEFGHIJKLMNOPQRSTUVWXYZ 1234567890 E≡

ABCDEFGHIJKLMNOPQRST E≡
UVWXYZ 1234567 89

ABCDEFGHIJKLMNOPQRSTUVWXYZ E≡
1234567890

ABCDEFGHIJKLMNOPQRSTU E≡
VWXYZ 1234567890

The Gettysburg Address

To practice your lettering, copy the total Gettysburg Address in a style of alphabet that you like. You develop the consistent style necessary for good lettering by practicing.

Fourscore and seven years ago our fathers brought forth on this continent a new nation, conceived in liberty, and dedicated to the proposition that all men are created equal. Now we are engaged in a great civil war, testing whether that nation, or any nation so conceived and so dedicated, can long endure. We are met on a great battlefield of that war. We have come to dedicate a portion of that field as a final resting place for those who here gave their lives that that nation might live. It is altogether fitting and proper that we should do this. But in a larger sense we cannot dedicate, we cannot consecrate, we cannot hallow this ground. The brave men, living and dead, who struggled here, have consecrated it far above our poor power to add or detract. The world will little note, nor long remember, what we say here; but it can never forget what they did here. It is for us, the living, rather to be dedicated here to the unfinished work which they who fought here have thus far so nobly advanced. It is rather for us to be here dedicated to the great task remaining before us, that from these honored dead we take increased devotion to that cause for which they gave the last full measure of devotion; that we here highly resolve that these dead shall not have died in vain; that this nation, under God, shall have a new birth of freedom, and that government of the people, by the people, and for the people, shall not perish from the earth.

☐ *Overlay a sheet of tracing paper and hand letter the Gettysburg Address using these guidelines. Your hand will get sore, but your lettering will greatly improve.*

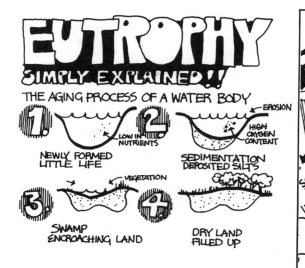

EUTROPHY
SIMPLY EXPLAINED!!
THE AGING PROCESS OF A WATER BODY

1 NEWLY FORMED LITTLE LIFE — LOW IN NUTRIENTS

2 SEDIMENTATION DEPOSITED SILTS — EROSION — HIGH OXYGEN CONTENT

3 SWAMP ENCROACHING LAND — VEGETATION

4 DRY LAND FILLED UP

The Influence of Letterforms

This page has examples of different kinds of lettering. Notice that each drawing has a different kind of letterform. The many styles do different things to each drawing giving the drawing a feeling consistent with the style of the letterform used. The key is for you to choose and draw the right one for the drawing.

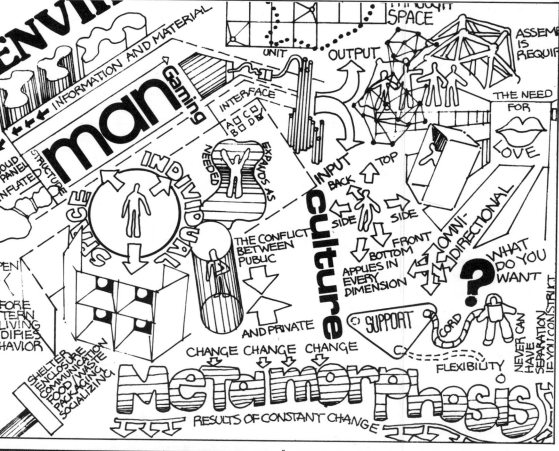

WHITE FORMICA TOP
¼" CUT
TEAK WOOD VENEER
OPEN UNIT

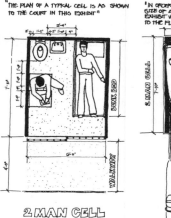

"THE PLAN OF A TYPICAL CELL IS AS SHOWN TO THE COURT IN THIS EXHIBIT"

2 MAN CELL

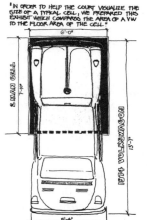

"IN ORDER TO HELP THE COURT VISUALIZE THE SIZE OF A TYPICAL CELL, WE PREPARED THIS EXHIBIT WHICH COMPARES THE AREA OF A VW TO THE FLOOR AREA OF THE CELL"

Conclusion

I have shown you how to simplify people, foliage, and letterforms. Other things can be simplified in the same fashion as these things were. For instance, an often seen object is an automobile. The inclusion of indicated automobiles may enhance your drawings.

Buildings, landscapes, and mechanical parts may also be things you want or need to indicate to make your drawings look better. You should learn how to indicate these additional objects in much the same way as you did people or foliage. Indicated objects are done simply and economically by drawing the critical shapes of the objects and using detail sparingly. Give indicated objects their essential form, but delete unnecessary detail.

Once these basic indications are learned they become *visual clichés* you can insert into your drawings easily. Using indication is a major method for improving your drawings and learning rapid visualization. Do you remember the story of the student who awed the other students with his ability to do drawings rapidly ? The story is one example of a common occurence. People not skilled at drawing cannot believe the speed and ability of people trained in rapid visualization. But all rapid viz

is really is drawing visual elements that you have drawn so many times it becomes second nature. What you draw are things you have drawn before—often things you have learned to indicate by simplifying the objects and omitting unneeded detail.

You Can't Drink from an Empty Bucket

You should have in your head perfected ways of indication for the objects you draw often. To try and originate some objects for each drawing is a waste of time. Develop a visual picture in your mind so that you can "rubber stamp" drawings easily. Develop this knowledge by collecting examples of other people's work from magazines and books. Use their drawings as a springboard to help you develop your own indicated objects. Notice the methods they use to simplify objects or give drawings "pizzaz." Use these same kinds of approaches to improve your drawings.

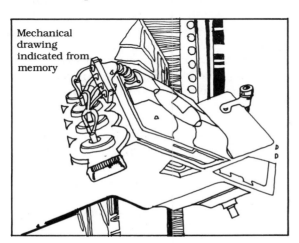

Mechanical drawing indicated from memory

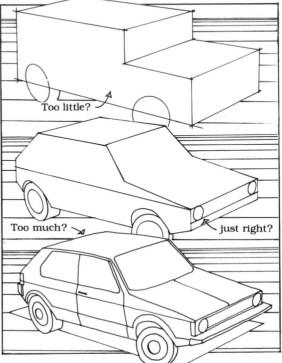

Too little?

Too much?   just right?

99

The Visualization Process

The process of evolving a thought, idea, concept, or image into a finished drawing is called *the visualization process*. This process is rapid development and refinement of an idea to a finished form. It involves definite steps and key concepts within each step that must be done if rapid viz is to work.

The common error among people is to think that they can go to the finished drawing without any intermediary steps. But one can't efficiently arrive at a finished drawing without going step by step together. It may seem strange, but step by step is the most efficient way.

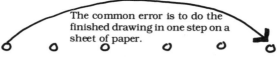

The common error is to do the finished drawing in one step on a sheet of paper.

The rapid viz process is key steps done rapidly on overlayed sheets of tracing paper.

An attempt to leap to the end of a finished drawing without progressively solving the problems along the way only creates more problems. I've seen students spend as many as 30 hours on a single drawing. They would erase and rework the drawing trying to make it right. They tried to make the leap from a half-formed idea to a finished form drawing. It seldom works. By rapidly doing each step—considering all the important points in each step—it is actually faster to finish a drawing.

Key Steps in the Rapid Viz Process

Evolve the drawing– The drawing evolves through successive layers of tracing paper. Each successive drawing is done quickly.

Overlay sheets– Use transparent sheets through which you can trace the best of the drawing underneath. Fix only what's wrong

from below. Let the best of the drawing float to the top; the bad parts sink out of sight.

Follow this sequence– Keep in control by going step by step to a better drawing. Each new tracing is obviously better—you know what's wrong below and you fix it on the sheet above. These are the things you improve as you proceed: whole to parts, known to unknown, simple to complex, coarse to refined, rough to finished, vague to clear, small to large.

Progressive levels of refinement and evolution
Best and last is at the top

Successive layers of tracing paper

Fix only what's wrong

Flow

Speed

When refining the drawing, speed is important. You should push yourself to draw as rapidly as possible. People learn to read faster by pushing themselves beyond their limits. They read very fast, often so fast that they do not comprehend, remember or understand what they are reading. But when they slow down again, they usually will slow down to a faster speed than where they started. That's the way it works here. You need to draw faster than you can do easily. When you slow down to your normal speed, you will find that your normal speed has actually increased somewhat. As you push yourself faster and faster, your speed gradually improves to the point where you can draw quickly and accurately.

Also, speed will improve your drawings. Your drawings look fresher as you learn to draw them more rapidly. Practice will help you draw faster. It will also help you improve the visual appearance of your drawings.

In the cold hard world of business, time is money. If you are an architect, engineer, designer, or whatever, the firm you work for will not keep you if you can't produce a good product quickly.

The graph shows a time efficiency curve. The message conveyed by the curve is that you get to a point in your drawings where it takes considerable time to gain any improvement. When you first start a drawing, every bit of time makes a great deal of improvement in the drawing. But as the drawing progresses to a more finished stage, it takes more and more time to make any visible improvement in the drawing. You need to learn when you have passed the point of efficiency—the point where you are spending too much time for the good derived. Stop when this happens. Don't overkill. Recognize your point of diminishing returns.

One way to guard against inefficient use of time is to determine in the beginning what is needed for your drawing. If you can accomplish your goal by drawing quickly on a scrap of paper, why do more? If detail is important to convey the idea, use detail. If detail is not necessary, then don't go to the bother of including unnecessary detail. You can become more efficient by deciding what is needed, drawing to that point, and not doing more.

The Visualization Process

The visualization process can be divided into 3 stages. A series of key concepts applies to each stage.

Stage 1 - Thumbnails

Here you make quick, small idea sketches. Thumbnails show very little detail. Their primary purpose is to set the stage for the final drawing by solving conceptual problems on a small scale. The thumbnail stage is a quick, rough sketch, done to scale but small—about the size of your thumb. You can solve many of the problems at thumbnail scale before going on to the next step. The key purposes or concepts you solve in this stage are:

—They are small so you can draw many until you find the best solution.
—Find the outer proportion, the best size for the drawing.
—Find the order of importance of the elements in the drawing.
—Determine the point of view.
—Solve negative/positive shape relationships.
—Become aware of the perceptual tendencies of the viewer toward your drawing.
—Solve value relationships by working from dark to light values.

Stage 2 - Transparencies

In this stage you make the first full-size sketch. Then, by tracing the drawing again and again, you evolve and correct the drawing. This transparent stage is where you work out the basic relationship between the parts. The following are the key concepts to accomplish in the transparent stage:

—First you transfer the drawing from the small thumbnail to the larger finished size.
—You begin with transparent shapes and evolve to actual drawing by tracing the drawing again and again.
—Determine emphasis and use detail, contrast and the like to emphasize those things you want emphasized.
—Add the necessary detail to the different elements in the drawing to make a finished drawing.
—Correct errors as you proceed from transparency to transparency.

Stage 3 - Final Drawing

To complete the drawing you make one last tracing. This time your emphasis is to give the drawing a freshness. Here you also strive for viewer involvement—the drawing must communicate your intent to the viewer. And last, you frame the drawing for final presentation if a frame is required. The key concepts you strive for in the final drawing are:

—The line weight should give a feel of freshness.
—Color is added if desired.
—Deliberately *backtrack* your drawing, which is to say that you deliberately leave some lines out, make portions more sketchy and loose, and make the drawing less refined so that the viewer can become more personally involved with the drawing.
—Make a final decision, depending upon the final context where the drawing will be seen and the purpose of the drawing, as to how the drawing will be presented to the viewer—does it need to be framed, colored, etc.?

Drawing Effectiveness Graph

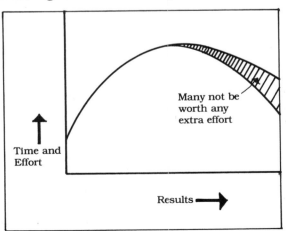

Many not be worth any extra effort

Time and Effort

Results

Stage 1—Thumbnails

Thumbnails are small drawings about the size of your thumb. They're done small, so that you can get the basic ideas, feelings, and relationships between the elements.

This thumbnail stage is where you visualize the key, central concepts—the basic idea of how you're going to put that drawing together. It's much easier to work at this small size to solve the problems while they're easy to solve than to try to solve problems at a much larger size. You should learn at this stage to play with things, to defer judgment, and to conceive many different thumbnail drawings, each one a further clarification of the previous one. Many decisions that are made here are critical ones; and it's much easier to solve problems here than on a big scale. Pictured here are some examples of

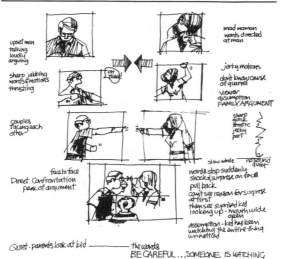

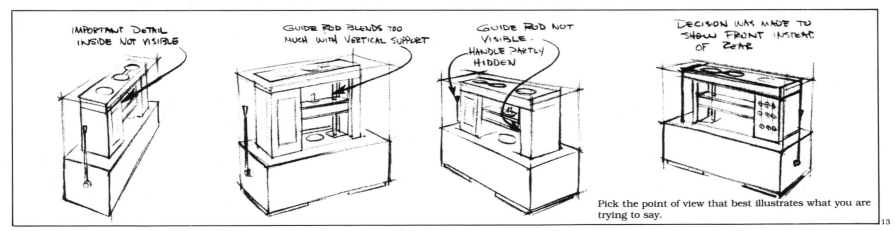

IMPORTANT DETAIL INSIDE NOT VISIBLE

GUIDE ROD BLENDS TOO MUCH WITH VERTICAL SUPPORT

GUIDE ROD NOT VISIBLE - HANDLE PARTLY HIDDEN

DECISION WAS MADE TO SHOW FRONT INSTEAD OF REAR

Pick the point of view that best illustrates what you are trying to say.

various areas where thumbnails have played a part in the development process.

These examples also show you the wide range that thumbnails can take.

Thumbnail—Key Concepts

As discussed earlier, there are several key concepts to think about and accomplish during the thumbnail stage of developing the drawing. Those key concepts were listed above; they are explained in more detail below.

Quantity

Since thumbnails are small, quickly drawn, conceptual drawings, you can draw many until you find a solution to your problem. The more ideas you can put on paper, the better your chance to find an appropriate solution.

The natural tendency is to start with typical solutions that should work and then proceed to more unique and outlandish solutions as you do more thumbnails. The best solutions often come in later thumbnails rather than in the early ones. Defer judgment. You need to have a mind free of prejudices in order to find a good solution. The more possibilities you can come up with, the greater your chance to find a

workable solution. And don't be afraid to combine ideas from many thumbnails into one good solution.

Outer Proportion (the drawing size)

First, let's consider the picture plane. The picture plane is the shape of the paper, the final overall proportion that you have to work with. It's a flat surface, through which the picture is seen. This plane establishes the comparative relationships with all other lines, planes, directions and movements within its borders. The picture plane is the basis for judging how the elements will work. The picture is limited entirely by this surface—it is a thing that you have to live with—a basic shape that dictates and sets the bounds for your drawing. This picture frame is the artificially frozen image you have to deal with. The shape of it affects what's in it. Your drawing will only look good if it is positioned correctly within the drawing area.

Order of Importance

You cannot emphasize all parts of the drawing. Some things are subordinate to other things. You have to decide which things are most

important in the drawing and which things are not as important. This order of importance determines how you will draw certain elements and where you will position things. I find that if I assign three levels of dominance in the drawing that I get the best results. One or two things are main points in a drawing—they are dominant. Other things are subordinate to the main elements. And last, other elements are subordinate to everything. In an earlier section I explained how to draw the subordinate elements; just remember to keep them simple and basic.

Point of View

Point of view is the position in space from where you view the image you plan to draw. Is the object at eye level, or above eye level or below eye level? You must decide this before you begin to draw.

Once you have decided eye level you must determine where to place elements within the drawing. As a general rule, we all have a natural visual preference for odd divisions of space over even divisions. One third seems to be much more pleasing than one half. This can be deliberately imposed on your drawing by dividing it into thirds and by putting the major elements, or points of emphasis, within those thirds.

A help for placing things in correct position in a drawing is to use a matrix. The matrix consists of hidden lines that nobody sees but are always there. The matrix is an unseen grid pattern. This grid pattern helps organize the elements of the drawing. By using the grid matrix to line up the elements, you give a cohesiveness to the whole drawing.

Since the purpose of the matrix is to give order to the drawing, be careful not to violate the matrix. But if you must break this matrix, break it for a good reason. The grid matrix gives an organized linear quality that's felt in all well done graphic presentations. Use the grid to control the drawing so that you can accomplish a particular goal that you are trying to reach in the drawing .

This is a sample of the grid matrix used for the layout of this book.

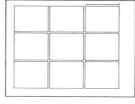

What do you see below? Two heads or a vase? One is a negative shape, the other is a positive shape.

104

Negative/Positive Shape Relationships

Shapes are either positive (dark) or negative (light). The positive is the one that is obvious to everybody. That's the picture of the human being or building or whatever. The negative shape is the one that isn't as obvious to most people—that's the lightness around the object. In order for a drawing to succeed, both negative and positive shapes must be interesting. The negative shape is probably most critical and is the most often neglected as you draw. Make the negative shape interesting. Indeed, make both the negative and the positive shapes interesting.

Value Relationships

I try to use four values in my drawings—dark, dark grey, light grey, and light. The best way to decide placement of the values is to begin with the darkest colors first and proceed to the light colors. Give the drawing punch by placing the darkest values next to the lightest values. It is important that you draw correct shading and shadows (discussed on pages 60-71) but you can alter reality in order to achieve a desired result. The placement of different values in the drawing determines the overall design of the drawing. Be careful to position values in the most interesting place. This will come with practice, but as you learn to place values remember to divide space in interesting patterns and to use values to emphasize things.

Perceptual Tendencies

People have natural perceptual tendencies— natural preferences for viewing things. It is not as confusing as it sounds at first. People naturally tend to see visual things in common patterns. They have a tendency to read things from left to right, the same way they are taught

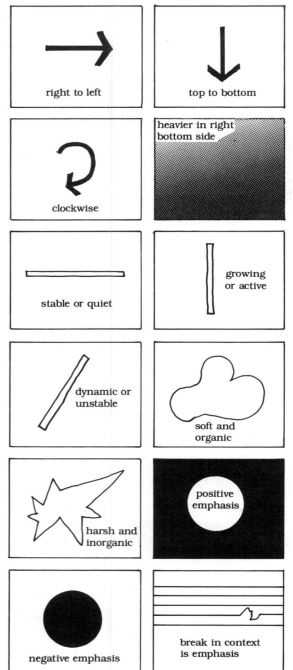

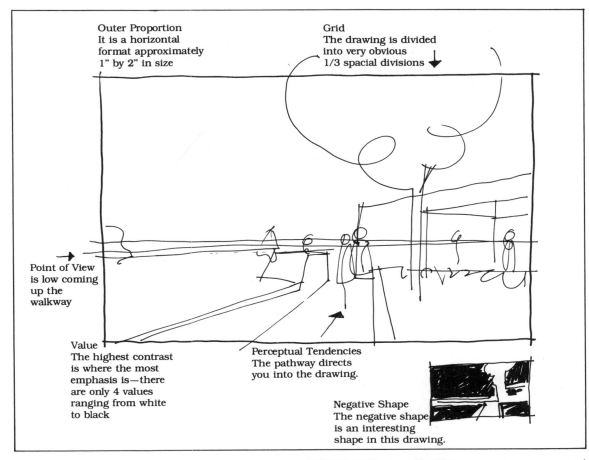

Outer Proportion
It is a horizontal
format approximately
1" by 2" in size

Grid
The drawing is divided
into very obvious
1/3 spacial divisions

Point of View
is low coming
up the
walkway

Value
The highest contrast
is where the most
emphasis is—there
are only 4 values
ranging from white
to black

Perceptual Tendencies
The pathway directs
you into the drawing.

Negative Shape
The negative shape
is an interesting
shape in this drawing.

The purpose of thumbnails is to solve as many problems as possible before moving to a more finished drawing. Thumbnails are very rough, consisting usually of splotches of light or dark in a small drawing. But by applying some very obvious principles at this early stage in the drawing process you can produce a better drawing quickly.

Exercises

The following exercises are designed to help you better understand and apply the skill of drawing thumbnails. If you don't want to do the exercises, turn to page 106.

☐ *Draw a thumbnail of any three of the items listed below. Your thumbnail should be no larger than 2" x 3".*

☐ *Draw and improve seven segments of what you consider the worst commercial on TV.*

☐ *An interior for the new "Burgereater" fast food restaurant near the university campus.*

☐ *A monument to be erected at the new underwater exposition to be held in 3 years.*

☐ *A new idea for city-wide bus stops complete with appealing landscaping.*

☐ *A modular mobile home exterior design.*

☐ *Five new ideas for a layout of your new business stationary.*

to read. Things are usually viewed from top to bottom. And if a circular pattern is used, people feel more comfortable seeing it in a clockwise direction.

Lines suggest various movements. Horizontal lines suggest a quiet, stable movement from left to right. The vertical line becomes very active, suggesting a movement from top to bottom. A diagonal line is dynamic. It feels like it's falling down and suggests danger and temporariness.

Be conscious of these, natural perceptual tendencies of people, so you can employ them in your drawing.

A dirigible docking to unload its cargo after a long voyage across the ocean.

Stage 2 - Transparencies Evolving the Drawing

The second stage of the drawing process is the transparency stage. It is during this stage that the drawing is evolved from the thumbnail sketch to a more finished form. In the thumbnail, all of the problems should be resolved on a small scale—especially those problems of design, division of space, negative and positive shapes, and the like. In this second stage we convert the thumbnail to the full scale size and we refine the drawing into a finished form.

Redraw Full Scale

The first step is to transfer to full scale. In doing this you need to make sure that the thumbnail is designed correctly. Once you know that everything is as it should be, then duplicate the rough form full scale. Rough out the thumbnail full size.

There are many ways to enlarge your thumbnail to full size. See page 46 for one method using a grid pattern.

One thing to remember is that you can not draw something if you do not know what it looks like. You can't drink from an empty cup. You can't draw from an empty head. If you don't have the image of what you are drawing firmly planted in your mind, then you must have an object, or image, to look at to aid you in drawing the object correctly.

Refine the Drawing

To this point you have transferred the thumbnail sketch to a full-size drawing. What you need to do now is to refine the drawing. Lay a transparent sheet on top of the drawing. Redraw the same thing again. It is much easier to refine by a transparent process than it is to erase and work over the original. When redraw-

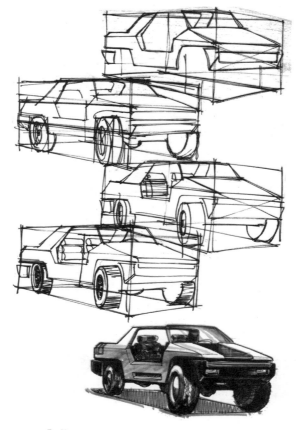

ing, you can drop out the things that you don't want, or retain and improve the things that you do want.

It could take only one transparent tracing after the full-scale blowup or it might take ten or twenty tries to get the drawing exactly right. It is easier and faster to redraw using transparent tracings than it is to rework the original.

Transparent Shapes

Once drawn full-scale, the next step is to correct the drawing. Define the basic shapes. You will have spheres, cubes, and cylinders

that are the beginnings of what they will eventually become—buildings, people, and so forth. Correct the perspective so that the appropriate lines converge at vanishing points, that the lines that should be parallel are parallel, and so forth. One way to make this drawing correct is to include the hidden lines that in the end will not show. What I mean by hidden lines are the edges, the corners and the sides of the building that will not be seen in the finished drawing. Draw the hidden lines as though the building, or whatever object, appears to be transparent—this allows you to be sure it is drawn correctly.

One thing to remember is there are certain essential points in any drawing. The corner of a building, or the point of a gable of a building, or the base of an electronic receiver are examples of these critical points in a drawing. They define the limits of what you are drawing. If you put an obstruction in front of one of these important points, it is difficult for the viewer to imagine how the object goes. It is important to have certain key points on the drawing exposed—do not cover those critical points that help the viewer understand what is happening in the drawing.

Emphasis

How do you emphasize those elements you want to be dominant? The basic principle of emphasis is to have something out of context. You emphasize things by making them different from the surroundings. Whatever is opposite of the surroundings is emphasized. For example, a circle among squares, a bump in a long straight line, a light speck against a dark surface, or detailed shapes against plain surfaces are all examples of something being emphasized. Change tends to attract our attention. These changes we call emphasis.

If the emphasis in a drawing is a certain building, for example, put your dark against lights there, and your details there. The points of change will draw attention and contribute to the viewer seeing that building.

Be careful to emphasize the essential points and de-emphasize those points that are nonessential. If a building is to be most important in your drawing, for example, give the building the details, give it the brightest colors, give it the most contrast, so that the viewer's attention is drawn to that building. The trees and the people and the surroundings of the building should be de-emphasized. They should not be as detailed, they should not be as contrasty, the colors should not be as exciting as the main building. De-emphasize secondary elements. Emphasize those things that you most want the viewer to see.

Show the best, most revealing, most interesting view of an object. In your drawing, are you showing the side of the building that tells the most about that building? Or is the part of the building you are showing not as interesting as it could be? Give the viewer the most interesting view of the object you are drawing that you can.

Errors

As you work with this drawing, it will become close to your heart. You probably will begin to overlook glaring and obvious mistakes because you are working so closely with it. I have drawn buildings before, for example, that to me looked just fine after I had worked on them for two or three hours. I have had people ask me why I had made such obvious mistakes. The building had walls that slanted, or other obvious mistakes. But, because I had become so attached to the drawing, I could not see those mistakes. You need to have a way to check your drawing to make sure that you have not made some outstanding errors.

One of the most effective ways to check for errors is to get another point of view from which to see your drawing. Here are some ways you can do that:

1. Turn your drawing upside-down.
2. Hold your drawing in front of a mirror.
3. Ask a friend to look at it.
4. Put your drawing across the room at a distance from you and look at the drawing.
5. Leave your drawing and then return to it a day or a week later—the lapse of time will enable you to look at the drawing with "new eyes."

Upon discovering mistakes in your drawing you will need to decide what warrants correcting and what is just overkill. If the mistake isn't important to the purpose of the drawing, you may not need to spend the time to fix it. If the the mistake detracts from the drawing, fix it.

When drawing things in three dimensions, keep in mind the following points:

1. Bigger things appear closer and smaller things appear farther away.
2. Place objects in front of, or behind, other objects so that overlapping occurs—this gives a more real feeling of depth.

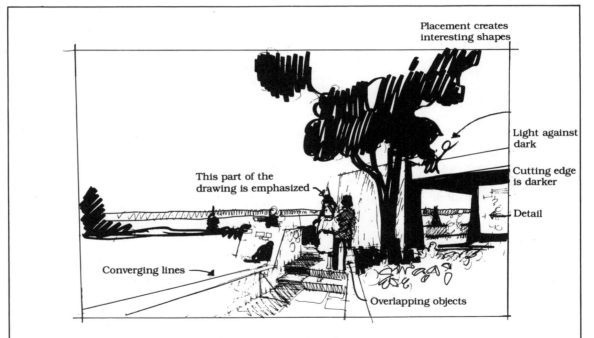

As you evolve this drawing through the different stages, you have worked it to make it more correct, but you may find that your drawing has that look of being overdone. This is one of the most common mistakes that people make as they begin to draw. They fiddle to the point that the drawing is overdone. I expect that, in the beginning, this will happen to you. That's all right, because in the next stage I will show you how to loosen up the drawing. I will show you how to get some viewer involvement with your drawing—how to give it more appeal. So don't worry about making it overdone at this stage. Worry about making it *correct*.

3. Lines converge in the distance as the objects go away from you.
4. Place a cutting edge around the outside edge of objects.

Stage 3 - The Final Drawing

This is the stage where you evolve the final drawing that the viewer will see. Some drawings will go through many transparencies and be quite elaborate before getting to this final stage—other drawings will get there rapidly.

Context

This final drawing needs to be refined in accordance with its use with the audience. This final drawing communicates with the viewer. The final touches that you put on should be done in accordance with the realization that this drawing must communicate. Like all communication you want it to be loose, free, and spontaneous as though you know exactly what you are doing and can freely and easily communicate with someone else. Remember that the value of the final drawing is its ability to communicate what you want communicated.

Color

You may determine that some color will help your line drawing. Remember to be selective, using color sparingly. A little color at strategic points should be sufficient. Line drawings, rapid viz drawings, don't need more than 3 colors—a bright color for the most important part of the drawing, a secondary color that complements the main color and is more subdued, and a third color that is very subdued. Don't be so splashy with color that your drawing looks like a circus (unless you are drawing a circus).

108

Backtrack—Developing Viewer Involvement

You have evolved your drawing and corrected your drawing so that it is complete and correct. You may want, however, to undo some of the drawing so that the viewer can become involved. You want the viewer to get the feeling that you did it rapidly in a few minutes, but very skillfully. You want your drawing to communicate rather than be "just another drawing."

You want your drawing to interact with the viewer. This way the viewer becomes a part of that drawing and becomes intensely involved with the drawing. One way to cause this to happen is to leave out details that the viewer must fill in from his own mind. Most people don't realize that they have a tendency to fill things in, but they do. You have heard the saying, "Roses are red, violets are...........;" you filled that in! The way you achieve viewer involvement in your drawing is to leave out little things here and there. Go back to your final drawing. You need to do one more drawing of it; you need to leave out lines, details, and other little things here and there. This will cause the viewer to become involved because he must fill in the details in his mind.

Look at the examples on pages 72-73. Try to determine what has been left out that the viewer is to fill in. Notice that the edges of buildings or trees or a lot of the different elements in the drawing are not complete. The edge doesn't go from top to bottom where you see every bit of it. There's nothing in front of that edge to block the view of it, but nonetheless it's not there. It's left blank for a reason, so that the viewer, you, will need to complete that drawing in your mind.

Matting

Once the drawing is totally finished you will need to mount it for your audience to see.

You've done the drawing on transparent tracing paper which needs a backup sheet for viewing.

The most common way to mount drawings is to cut a window out of matte board and fix the drawing behind the window. I *do not* recommend this method unless you intend to show the drawing over and over again.

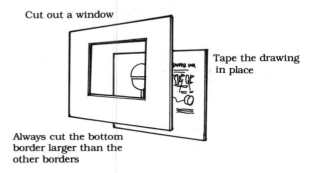

Cut out a window

Tape the drawing in place

Always cut the bottom border larger than the other borders

Here are some other ways I prefer for mounting the final drawing. These methods are faster and cheaper and they look just as nice for most situations.

The easiest method is to draw a very bold line around the outer edge of the drawing. Then simply adhere the drawing to an opaque piece of paper using staples, tape, or the like.

Or you can adhere your drawing to a piece of matte board. Use spray adhesive or black photo tape. Around the edge of the drawing place black tape to form a border (you can find the tape in a photo store). Last, cut the matte board to size.

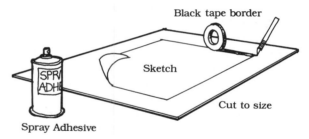

Black tape border

Sketch

Cut to size

Spray Adhesive

Line Quality

Another element that helps bring the final drawing to the quality you want is to use different densities of lines. You should use at least three kinds of lines within your drawing. You should have some lines that are hard, thick, dark lines. You should have some lines that are medium. You should have some lines that are very light and very faint. Three different line thicknesses make your drawing more lively and more interesting.

These drawings show the use of various weights of line to improve their impact.

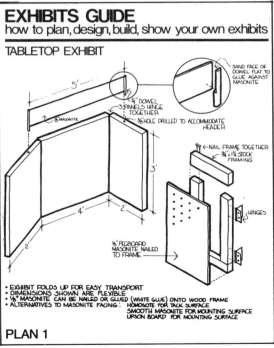

EXHIBITS GUIDE
how to plan, design, build, show your own exhibits

TABLETOP EXHIBIT

5'

⅛" MASONITE

¼" DOWEL
3 PANELS HINGE
TOGETHER

⅜" HOLE DRILLED TO ACCOMMODATE
HEADER

SAND FACE OF
DOWEL FLAT TO
GLUE AGAINST
MASONITE

← NAIL FRAME TOGETHER
¾" × 1¼ STOCK
FRAMING

3'

4'   2'

2'

← HINGES

⅛" PEGBOARD
MASONITE NAILED
TO FRAME

• EXHIBIT FOLDS UP FOR EASY TRANSPORT
• DIMENSIONS SHOWN ARE FLEXIBLE
• ⅛" MASONITE CAN BE NAILED OR GLUED (WHITE GLUE) ONTO WOOD FRAME
• ALTERNATIVES TO MASONITE FACING: HOMOSOTE FOR TACK SURFACE
                                    SMOOTH MASONITE FOR MOUNTING SURFACE
                                    UPSON BOARD FOR MOUNTING SURFACE

PLAN 1

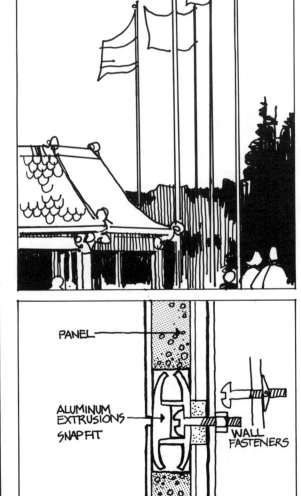

PANEL

ALUMINUM
EXTRUSIONS

SNAP FIT

WALL
FASTENERS

109

The Finished Drawing

The very last thing for a final drawing is to make sure that the drawing is presented under the right conditions. Make sure that the style of the drawing fits the situation in which you present it. If the drawing needs to be finished, make sure you have a finished drawing. If it needs to be rough and very spontaneous, then make your drawing sketchy and rough.

Try to foresee the circumstance where the drawing will be viewed. If it is a planning meeting for a building committee, for example, you may want to keep the drawing sketchy and loose so that the people don't incorrectly assume that you have made final design decisions when you don't have the authority to do so.

When showing this last drawing, make sure it is of adequate size and placed in the right position. If you are showing it fifty feet away, you can't use an 8 1/2 x 11 sheet; it must be a much larger drawing. Similarly, if you are showing that drawing to kindergarten students, you wouldn't hang it seven feet high on the wall which is three or four feet above the eye level of those kindergarten students. Make sure that the drawing is placed correctly for the viewer to see.

I have seldom, if ever, completed a drawing that I thought was good enough. The feeling is there that something could have been done better—something could have been improved. But there comes a point where there is no time or desire to do more. I have to quit a particular drawing and go on to other things. You will probably have similar feelings—that it could be done better. Don't worry, it's normal to feel that way. Keep trying because with time your abilities will improve.

We Are All Salespersons

Have you ever thought about the fact that we are all salesmen every day of our lives? As we

110

The Finished Drawing

Notice areas where lines are left out—this will loosen a tight drawing.

meet someone else or talk to someone else we sell ourselves. We create an image or a concept in their minds about us. We are in fact salespersons. The more concisely, the more accurately, the more clearly, that we can present information to another individual, the better off we are.

Using strong visuals is one of the best ways to present things clearly to others.

Let me give an example of an architect friend and how rapid visualization benefited him in his business. This architect friend has created a large company that does architectural renderings for various architectural firms throughout the nation. He attributes the growth of his company largely to the fact that he can go into an architect's office and convince the architect that a strong visual presentation of the proposed building will aid the architect. If that architect can show the client what that building is going to look like, there is a lot better chance of doing a good job for the client. My friend claims that his ability to rapidly visualize a building, in essence, to speak in visuals, to the architect, aids him in landing work. As he talks to an architect about the importance of showing a client the building, my friend can draw out what he is talking about. As he draws it quickly before the architect's eyes, he gets a client; he sells a service. Using the same principle, if an architect can rapidly visualize before the client's eyes, then the architect can sell a service.

No matter what line of work we are in, no matter what relationship we have with someone else, if we can communicate a clear, concise message—if we can present ourselves and our concepts well and easily, then we are better off. Rapid viz allows us to do that.

Consider Your Audience

When creating visuals for communicating or presenting an idea, consider the audience care-

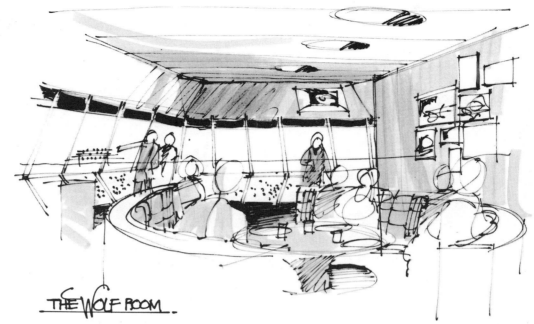

THE WOLF ROOM

fully. Who is the audience? Why are they there? What do you want them to know? What do they need to know? How are you going to tell them? Why should they know it? Answer all of those questions. Then make your visuals in accordance with the audience. Don't draw what *you* want to see—draw what *they* want to see. If you don't consider your audience, a visual presentation doesn't work.

Let me give an example. Shown below is a visual of a man putting rocks into a mining car. This visual was used in Africa. It didn't work. What it was supposed to do was to tell workers in a mine that as they saw debris on the track, they were to pick up the debris, put it in a cart, and haul it away. But the native mineworkers were used to reading things from

the opposite direction which was their native custom. The result was that the tracks became cluttered with debris because the workers thought that what was meant by the visual was to gather up the rocks, take the rocks to the tracks, put them on the tracks, and leave them there. The visuals were drawn from the point of view of the communicator, not from the point of view of the audience.

When using visuals in a presentation, always do it from the point of view of the audience. That is most important.

Rapid Viz—A Means to an End

Remember one thing: The visuals used in presentation are means to an end. We use those visuals to communicate a message or concept. They are not an end in themselves. Visuals are not meant to be hung on a wall or in a gallery for other people to see or to last forever. They are meant as a means of communicating.

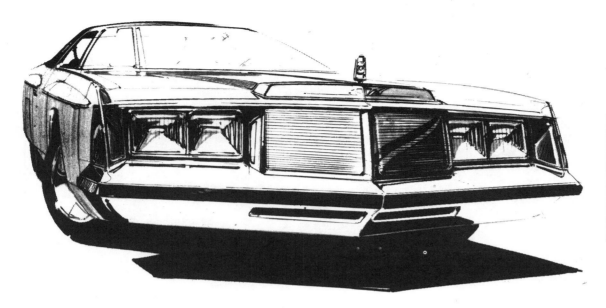

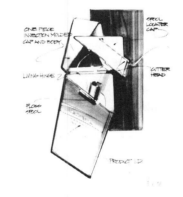

Summary

Remember that visuals are a means to an end. They are not an end in itself. Draw visuals that get a reaction—that cause something to happen—that produce the results that you want. Don't waste time and effort making a beautiful drawing. That well-done drawing, because of its beauty and the fact that it's so well done, may actually detract from the presentation. Use drawings that are a means to an end, drawings that accomplish a result. The drawing itself is not important. The act of communication, the conveyance of concepts that the drawing presents, is what is important.

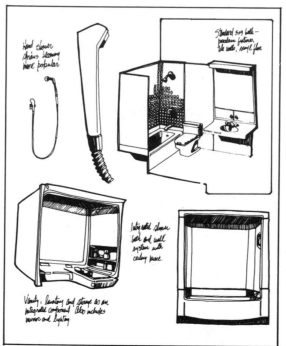

112

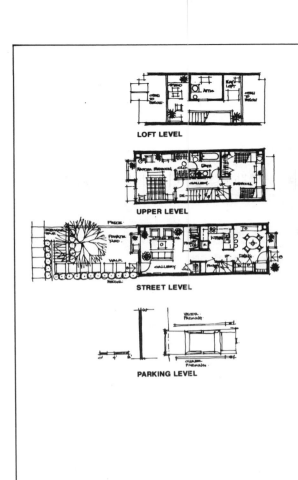

LOFT LEVEL

UPPER LEVEL

STREET LEVEL

PARKING LEVEL

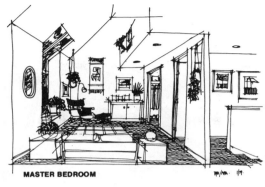

MASTER BEDROOM

**Architects/PlannersAlliance
Incorporated**

Ralph Folland Evans   AIA

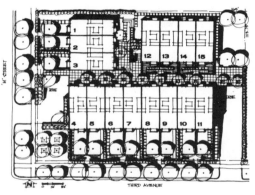

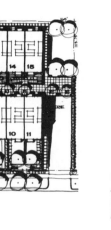

MASTER SITE PLAN

LIVING ROOM

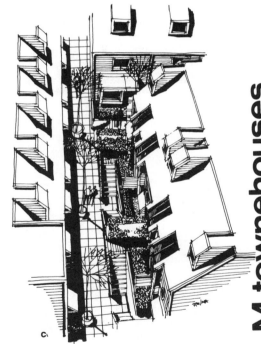

3rd & M townehouses

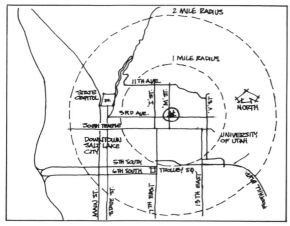

2 MILE RADIUS

1 MILE RADIUS

17

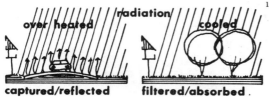

radiation

over heated

cooled

captured/reflected

filtered/absorbed.

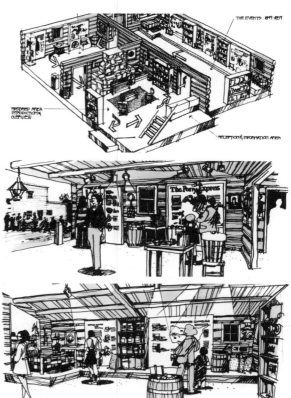

114

Graphic Expression

How important is it to learn to refine and expand visual potential? It's vital.

The mind thinks in pictures. It "sees" things. Where most of us fall short is in our ability to express these visual images. It follows that if we could learn to refine and express our visual abilities, we could benefit greatly.

In this section, I hope to show you how visual abilities can be refined through "graphic expression." Graphic expression is the conversion of thoughts, ideas, or concepts into symbols that have meaning. We all use graphic expression throughout life. We all use symbols to express thoughts and concepts. For example, the four symbols shown below symbolize "a transparent, odorless, tasteless liquid, a compound of hydrogen and oxygen, which constitutes rain, oceans, lakes, and rivers." You knew what we were talking about just from looking at the symbols—the word, the drawing, the chemical formula, the molecular model—they all represent the concept of a liquid we call water.

What you probably don't do, however, is to get the most out of the symbols you use. What I hope to show you is how to get more out of symbolic expression (graphic expression) of your thoughts. I hope to show you ways to use graphic symbols to help you learn, create, and communicate.

And one major new thing I hope to show you is how to create new graphic symbols. You've never been exposed to that before. How do you make a new symbol, all your own, that expresses what you want expressed? How do you develop new symbols that no one has ever created before, symbols that work well? I hope to give you some insight into how it's done.

Graphic expression, unfortunately, is not taught in school as is writing, but graphic expression does have just as widespread use as does writing. It is easier to draw a map than it is to write out in words all that a map can show graphically. The more you use graphic expression the more freedom and ease you will have in expressing yourself.

Expanding Your Symbolic Potential

But you already knew that. You use symbols all the time. So I'm not going to show you anything new about using symbols.

New Symbols

When you express yourself graphically, each thought, each concept, each message has its own set of symbols. Since most people don't

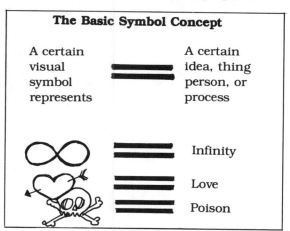

The Basic Symbol Concept

A certain visual symbol represents — A certain idea, thing person, or process

∞ — Infinity

Love

Poison

learn how to make symbols, they have difficulty expressing themselves graphically. So one of the first things that you need to learn is how to make symbols. You must learn how to give meaning to symbols so that when other people see your symbols, they understand what's happening.

Applying Graphic Expression

Once you have mastered how to make graphic symbols the use of graphic expression begins to be helpful for three basic things. Graphic expression is a great way to communicate clear, concise messages. Graphic expression is a tool to aid in learning and remembering. And graphic expression expands the mind so that creative potentials are realized and can inspire creative thinking. Let's talk about communication first.

Communicating

Remember that graphic symbols on maps allow maps to be more easily understood. Well, similar kinds of graphically expressed symbols make other concepts easy to communicate. It is sometimes much easier to communicate simple concise concepts through graphic symbols than it is through written words. A picture ofttimes really is worth a thousand words.

Since the mind sees visual images and patterns, if you can create visual patterns on paper, you can learn and remember more easily. It's usually easier to remember an illustration in a book, for example, than it is to remember a written concept you read somewhere in the hundreds of pages of material.

An example of the use of graphic symbols is the blueprint for a building. Graphic symbols are used to help the architect conceive the idea for the structure of the building. The same graphic symbols are used to communicate to the contractor how to build the newly created

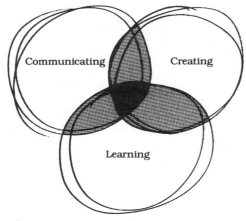

Graphic expression is used for all three processes.

structure. And finally, the carpenter uses blueprints to remember and recall the necessary instructions for building the structure correctly.

Learning and Recall

Have you ever gone someplace and sometime later had someone ask you how to get there? You close your eyes and you think for a minute: you can see the picture of the store or the destination in your mind. You know exactly what it looks like but you just can't remember the exact route to get there. You hop in your car and you start to go to this destination. As you pass the landmarks along the way the picture comes back in your mind and you remember again exactly where you are going and what route to take. And you can draw a map.

The mind has a tendency to learn and recall visually. Therefore, graphic expression is a way of extending the mind's ability to learn and remember more things.

Creativity

The third thing that graphic expression does is to expand the creative potential of the mind.

Thoughts are fleeting; they flash into the mind and then they disappear just as rapidly. Since creative thoughts are so fleeting, they don't seem to be real and are often lost. If you take those same thoughts and tie them to a piece of paper, they become real. You see them and they remain. You see them in detail. By capturing flashes of creative thoughts, much of the creative potential of the brain can be captured. If thoughts are not nailed down to a piece of paper they are easily lost forever.

Also, since the mind thinks visually, a way to talk to the mind is by graphically refining thoughts. Graphically rendering the thoughts makes it easier to refine or change the thoughts so they become better and more concrete. This is done by graphically writing them down, not only in verbal forms but also in picture forms, symbols of what the mind is thinking.

How to Become Better at Graphic Expression

There are three major points that help people learn how to express themselves graphically.

1. Choosing an appropriate symbol.
2. Deciding the level of abstraction.
3. Finding the essence of the concept that is to be graphically expressed.

1. Choosing the Appropriate Symbol

The first step to improving graphic expression is to choose the appropriate symbols. Symbols are ways of expressing one's thoughts. Every different concept has a different kind of symbol to best express the concept. You must learn to choose appropriate symbols that convey what the concept is. Many examples of symbols are shown here—poisonous materials, a locked or unlocked chain, do not smoke, do not feed the bears, open or shut, on or off, fast or slow.

117

To choose the appropriate symbol that expresses your thought, since there are many different ways of expressing any thought, determine a purpose on which to base the meaning of your symbol. If you want to express that something is *deadly poisonous,* then it is appropriate to have the skull and crossbones. If you want a different meaning for the same poisonous material, i.e., you want to communicate that poisonous materials should be stored in closed bottles, you have changed the purpose. This causes you to change the symbol—to graphically say something different. So the symbol is dependent upon your purpose.

Notice on the bottom of the matrix on the next page—the matrix with the eye. There are many different points of view about that eye. Each one of those different illustrations on the bottom reveals a different point of view about the same subject matter, the eye. Notice that as the point of view changes, so does the graphic symbol that is used. This is what we mean by letting the point of view dictate the appropriate symbol.

2. The Level of Abstraction

You must decide the level of abstraction. What this means is that a symbol, to be effective, can be very realistic or very abstract. Sometimes it is more helpful to have the symbol be very realistic. Sometimes it is better to have it be very abstract. Look at the matrix on the eye again. At the bottom left is a photo of a real eye. You know exactly what it is. As you proceed upward, notice that the eye becomes sketchier until it becomes just a dot. That dot means "an eye" just as the photo below does. If, for example, you use a photograph for an eye in a cartoon character, it looks out of place. It doesn't say any more about the character having an eye than does a single dot. And, in fact,

118

a single dot looks better and seems more appropriate on a cartoon.

The same happens with other kinds of symbols. Sometimes symbols are too realistic, too complex. Simple, abstract symbols, can serve well depending upon the context.

Some laws govern levels of abstraction. One is that the more abstract a symbol becomes, the more manageable it is. The symbol can be applied to a lot of different situations. The more abstract something is, the harder it is to understand and the more it depends upon its surroundings or its context to give that abstract symbol meaning. That one single dot, which is an abstract symbol for an eye as shown on the matrix, could be used as an eye for a variety of cartoon characters. A more photographic eye, however, is more real, is more concrete, and is less manageable. It would fit on only one specific face and look good.

On the other hand, the more concrete or realistic in its application a symbol is, the more concrete and limited in its application is our understanding. You know more about the eye that is more carefully drawn or illustrated than you do about the dot. Concrete, realistic symbols are more understandable; they don't rely on outside situations or context to bring the full meaning out.

Find the Essence

Graphic symbols have an essence of meaning. Once you find that essence of meaning it can become the basis for creating the graphic symbol. An example of finding the graphic symbol that carries the essence is shown in the flowers, the crosses and structures that you see here. You'll notice that all of these symbols have a similar pattern of a double cross laid at an angle. The graphic essence of expression in all of those symbols is the same—the double cross.

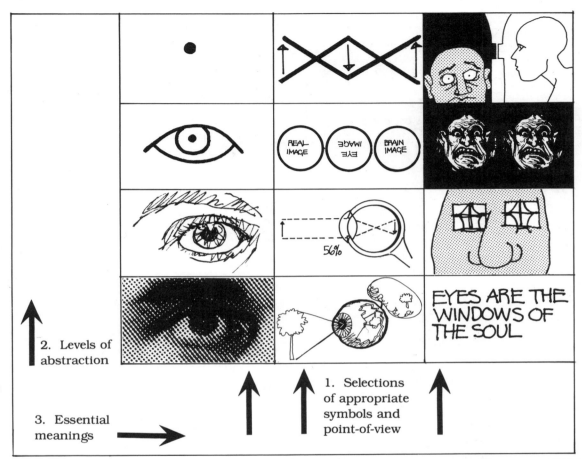

2. Levels of abstraction

3. Essential meanings

1. Selections of appropriate symbols and point-of-view

Look at the graph on this page showing how the lens of the eye inverts images. It shows how the eye functions. The top symbol of x's and arrows in this diagram of the eye is a graphic symbol showing inversion. You strip it back to its essence, its meaning, and you discover that an 'x' indicates "inversion." Once you get back to that basic symbol for inversion you could create some other illustrations that show inversion by using that same 'x' as the underlying structure.

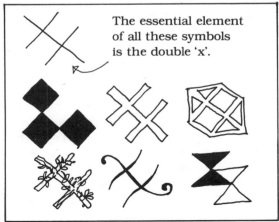

The essential element of all these symbols is the double 'x'.

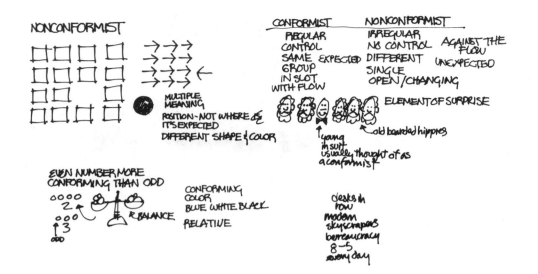

The finished drawing here used essential concepts to communicate nonconformity.
—One window in the building is done different from the rest.
—The texture of the window is different.
—The man below is going in a different direction.
—The dress of all the businessmen is the same, except for the lone man.
—The body size is different.
—The way of walking is different.

Creating Graphic Symbols

Now let's create a graphic symbol so that you can see how it is done. Take the concept of a non-conformist. First of all, write all of the things that a conformist is. A conformist is regular, controlled, the same as someone else. A group of many people that are alike would be an example of conformity. Some examples of conformists, or things that conform, would be a group of businessmen in suits, ties, and coats, a school of fish in the ocean all swimming in the same way, a string of windows in a skyscraper where every window is exactly the same, a bunch of hippies all dressed alike, and so on.

What is a non-conformist? By definition, a non-conformist is irregular, he is the opposite of a conformist. He would be uncontrolled or uncontrollable. He would be different in some way from other people or would behave differently. He would behave as an individual rather than as a member of a group.

Now that we have defined what a conformist is and what a non-conformist is, we have stripped back the concept of a non-conformist to the essential meaning that is to be graphically symbolized.

Above are examples of conformity/nonconformity: the building with all the windows the same, except for one where someone is poking his head out between the drapes; the businessmen walking down the road, all dressed the same except that one person is going the wrong direction; the squares except for one round thing; the arrows all going the same direction except for one that's not.

Notice the element of surprise. You would normally expect that in the row of businessmen with a single non-conformist the non-conformist would be the hippie. But if you put hippies in a row and have one conservative businessman, then the conservative businessman becomes the (surprise) non-conformist.

With practice you can create graphic symbols. Since you are not accustomed to doing it now, at first you may encounter some difficulty creating the appropriate symbol. Remember the following when striving for that symbolic meaning to best describe the concept you wish to describe:

1. Let your determined point of view help dictate the appropriate symbol.
2. Determine the level of abstraction needed. If your symbol must be very understandable then choose a realistic symbol. If your symbol must apply to many situations, and it must have general application for a variety of situations, then choose a more abstract symbol.
3. Find the essence of the concept in order to find the correct symbol. Strip the concept back to its basic meaning so that you can find a symbol to recreate the same meaning.

Do the following exercises.

☐ *Match the terms below with the correct symbols shown on page 118. Write the number in the blank spot.*

____ Bell Telephone logo
____ Poison
____ America
____ Stop your car
____ Fast/slow
____ Look to the right
____ Remove
____ Half full
____ Don't feed the bears
____ Locked/unlocked
____ Dollars
____ Male/female
____ North
____ Ancient Indian symbol
____ Clockwise
____ Sign language
____ Backpacking
____ A hobo symbol meaning "a kind lady lives here"
____ Fire prevention
____ Sixteenth note
____ Ranger station
____ Resistor

☐ *Make a grid of other senses similar to the grid for seeing shown on page 119.*
Hearing
Smelling
Touch
Taste

Use these points of view to express characteristics.
Visually express the *function* of the sense.
Visually express the *form* of the sense.
Visually express an *attribute* of the sense.

☐ *Visually express five of the following sayings:*
Politics makes strange bedfellows
Taken with a grain of salt
Not what it is all cracked up to be
Pay through the nose
March to the beat of a different drummer
Whole ball of wax
The show must go on .
Paddle your own canoe
Out of the frying pan, into the fire
Leave no stone unturned
It's no skin off my tail

☐ *Visually illustrate two of the following concepts:*
Influential
Polarity
Obstinate
Self-actualization
Counter culture
Thinking
Security
Meaningless
Reciprocity
Recoil
Oneness
Sullen indifference

☐ *Create a symbol for a sign to communicate three of the following concepts:*
Poison
Don't open
Hospital zone
Unplug
Sleeping permitted
Camping permitted
Turn left
Must be accompanied by an adult
Beware of undertow

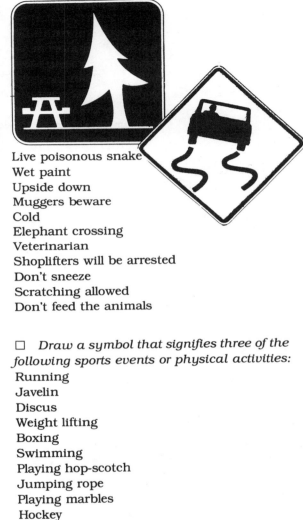

Live poisonous snake
Wet paint
Upside down
Muggers beware
Cold
Elephant crossing
Veterinarian
Shoplifters will be arrested
Don't sneeze
Scratching allowed
Don't feed the animals

☐ *Draw a symbol that signifies three of the following sports events or physical activities:*
Running
Javelin
Discus
Weight lifting
Boxing
Swimming
Playing hop-scotch
Jumping rope
Playing marbles
Hockey

Graphic Creation

It's important—yes, essential—that we become more visual. Our society is dominated by verbal thinking. We learn alphabets, words, and numbers in school. Art and drawing are played down as being less important. But everything—every machine, every invention, every modern convenience—existed first as a visual thought in someone's mind. Consider how important visual thinking really is. We owe our modern luxurious life to visual thinking. Doesn't it seem logical that we ought to learn to expand the creative visual potential inside all of us?

The next time you watch TV or flip a light switch or ride in an automobile remember that you are able to do it because someone before you *visualized* it in their mind. And not only did they visualize it, but they converted the visual thought into reality. It is mind-boggling to think that the world runs on visual images from people's minds.

How do you expand your creative potential? One proven effective method is to expand your visual potential. Rapid visualization expands visual potential. I want also to tell you some other ways of expanding creative potential. Remember, however, that creativity is enhanced by visual thinking and visual expression such as afforded by learning rapid visualization.

Ideas Don't Come from Nothing

There is no such thing as a creative idea that originates from nothing. Ideas come from the mind. And a mind filled with knowledge, experiences, and an acute observation of the surrounding world is more apt to bring forth creative ideas.

One major problem with creative ideas is that since ideas are only thoughts in the beginning, they are easily lost. In order to "keep" those ideas, those thoughts, it's important to commit to a piece of paper. Once drawn or written down, the ideas are saved. Once on paper, the ideas can be properly evaluated, refined, and improved. Get things down on paper.

Let's talk about ideas and how we start them coming.

Imagination

The greatest source of ideas is in our heads. The artist tends to use his sensory organs (eyes and ears principally) to soak up impressions about life. This bank of ideas can be recalled whenever needed. When this memory is fortified with strong art skills, the outflow of responses can be enhanced.

Learning to work this memory bank in a creative way is the biggest and most important challenge. Being confident, you can tackle themes or subject matter with enthusiasm, and find that sketching ability pays off in fruitful production. Again, remember that this kind of sketching, this rapid visualization of ideas, trades accuracy and detail for expressiveness. You are not drawing to create a photo-like copy; you are drawing sketchy, loose drawings that help you come up with or refine ideas. Idea drawing may be nothing more than lines that have meaning to you, but are meaningless to someone else looking at them. You may miss on the details but strike it rich on creative solutions. You can draw more spontaneously and occasionally recklessly.

Although at first you may feel wobbly in tackling a piece of white paper, once you get seriously involved (that means numerous efforts) the creative juices flow and you learn to trust both your memory and imaginative capacities. Drawings may be quite simple. Just working with abstract shapes and patterns may serve your purpose (the scribbles around the edge of your phone book reflect this type of improvised doodling). You may just repeat a single subject idea in different fashions.

Most important of all is to practice this imaginative play sketching with a pencil. Tie your mind to a problem.

What is a creative idea?

Creative ideas are rarely new—they are just old concepts combined in a new and useful way. The electric toothbrush is just an electric motor and a toothbrush. Ben Franklin made the first bifocal by combining two lenses in one pair of glasses. The telephone is a combination of Alexander Graham Bell's knowledge of the human ear coupled with magnetism and electricity.

All creative ideas are logical connections. Sometimes these connections seem irrational or illogical to an outside observer, but they are logical connections to the creator of the idea. If someone said, for example, that marbles are very similar to oil, you might laugh. But if you envision lubricating oil as millions of tiny marbles sandwiched between two surfaces you can see the logical similarity.

Making logical connections between objects is easier at abstract levels than at real levels. Liquid oil is not like a solid glass marble. But if you understand that, abstractly, oil often behaves as tiny beads of fluid, then it is easy to make the logical connection.

The V's illustrated below visually explain how abstraction helps create logical relationships. A snail and a man have nothing in common at the concrete level depicted by the bottom of the V. A man is completely different from a snail. But as you compare them in more general or more abstract terms, they have more things in common.

Any object can be compared to any other object from an abstract point of view. Pick two objects and try it—you will see for yourself.

Using abstraction might prove to be one of the most productive idea-getting thought processes you could ever master.

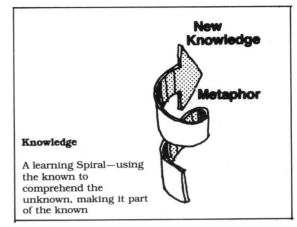

Knowledge

A learning Spiral—using the known to comprehend the unknown, making it part of the known

The Metaphor

Human beings need order in their lives. We seek an understandable framework on which to fasten new ideas and experiences. We understand the new by linking it with our knowledge of the past.

A metaphor is the comparison of the meaning and attributes of one thing to the meaning and attributes of something else.

Here are some examples:

Grandma is a real brick.
Changing his attitude is like moving a boulder.
The larger the island of knowledge, the longer the shore of wonder.

Metaphors can seem absurd at first, until the relationship is clear. How is friendship like a planet? We survive on the earth balanced between centrifugal force throwing us out and gravity holding us down. Friendship also ranges from being pulled too close and being thrown apart.

To learn from a metaphor, the learner must take charge; he must act and make some decision, take some risk. He does not manipulate, but invests something of himself, so that growth may result.

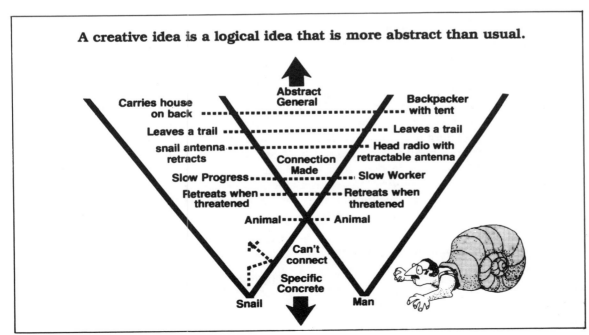

A creative idea is a logical idea that is more abstract than usual.

Abstract General

Carries house on back ---- Backpacker with tent
Leaves a trail ---- Leaves a trail
snail antenna retracts ---- Head radio with retractable antenna
Connection Made
Slow Progress ---- Slow Worker
Retreats when threatened ---- Retreats when threatened
Animal ---- Animal
Can't connect
Specific Concrete
Snail   Man

123

The Process of
Using Metaphors
To Form
New Ideas

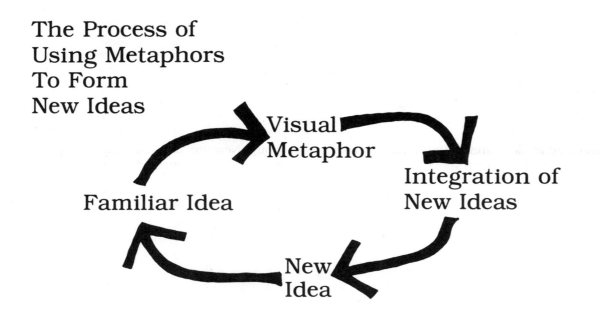

Visual Metaphor

Integration of New Ideas

Familiar Idea

New Idea

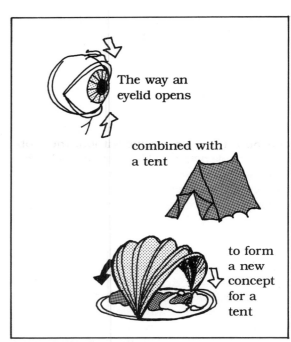

The way an eyelid opens

combined with a tent

to form a new concept for a tent

19

A new idea from an old metaphor

Lord Rutherford, after analyzing the data relevant to the structure of the atom, sought a model of the system he had discovered and found it in the solar system. Later experiments modified Rutherford's metaphor about the atom as a microscopic solar system, next using a metaphor of shells to understand the atom's structure. As knowledge advanced, the metaphor changed—scientists still needed some metaphor for comprehension—first the solar system, then shells, and who knows what next?

The metaphor is often used to decribe the emotions by comparing them with the physical world. Shakespeare penned, "Shall I compare thee to a summer's day?" and Victor Hugo wrote, "Laughter is the sun that drives winter from the human face."

Use a metaphor to generate new meaning from old or unfamiliar concepts. Put the words *"is like"* between things to create new relationships.

Visual metaphors are essential to many professions for the creation of ideas. An architect, for example, must rely on visual metaphors to create new buildings. Just as Shakespeare used verbal metaphors to add life and give interest to his plays, visual metaphors are used by the architect to give life and interest to a building. Frank Lloyd Wright, considered by many to be the greatest architect of this century, used metaphors to create his unsurpassed buildings. Hallways would burst into the freedom and light of a spacious room, giving a feeling of security and warmth. Shapes for buildings were patterned after shapes in nature. Room configurations were arranged so as to create certain feelings for the inhabitants of Wright's buildings.

Collective Creativity—For Groups or Individuals

Problem solving in a group can be very productive. This kind of collective problem solving is often referred to as "brainstorming." Actually, the creative methods that produce results, when a group of people collectively brainstorm a problem, are methods that also work well for individuals.

Rapid visualization helps refine ideas. The brainstorming methods explained in the following paragraphs will produce creative results. Your ability to express these creative solutions in some visual form on paper is essential to the refining of the embryonic ideas. Use rapid visualization to express the ideas. It will be faster and easier than trying to verbalize many of the creative expressions.

Rules for Finding Creative Solutions

Creative solutions can be made to happen by applying certain methods. If we can cause our minds to think in ways that produce creative new ideas, we will logically be more creative. The following are some "rules" that govern

124

creativity. If you follow the rules, you can be assured that your ability to come up with creative solutions will be increased.

1. State your problem.

The development of new ideas usually comes when you have a problem—a need that must be met. Jonas Salk would not have developed the polio vaccine without the problem of people dying and being crippled by that disease. And before he could cure polio, he had to find out what was *causing* it—he had to *know* the problem before he could solve it.

A local supermarket had a contest in which the prize was three minutes' shopping—the winners could load up their shopping carts with whatever they wanted, free, for that long.

The two winners showed two entirely different approaches. One spent hours before the contest walking around the store and deciding what she wanted, where it was, and how she could fit it in her cart. The other winner arrived just before the contest began.

When the gun sounded, the two winners took off racing down the aisle with carts in hand and food flying everywhere. When the race was over, it was easy to see who was the big winner. The woman who knew what she was looking for, where she could find it, and how she could get it had the most in her shopping cart. Searching for a good idea is like

winning three minutes' worth of free shopping, but the rewards are much greater than a can of soup or a frozen turkey. You can't expect to be the big winner if you aren't adequately prepared. You can't expect to land a good idea if you have no concept of what to hunt for and where to find it.

Put your problem down on paper. Once it's recorded in black and white, you can't make it go away just by forgetting it.

State the real problem. Don't be misled by preconceived notions. For example, many people tried to solve the housekeeper's problem of cleaning dirty floors by improving the broom. But only H. G. Booth realized that the problem was not poorly designed brooms—it was removing dirt. And so he threw out the broom and invented the vacuum cleaner which reversed wind to suck up dirt.

How a problem is stated exerts tremendous control over how it is solved. The definition of a problem can dictate a solution before creative thinking even begins. Be like H. G. Booth—don't confine yourself by trying to improve old methods that don't work well—get to the *real* problem and forget the same old solutions that have been tried a dozen times before.

2. Pick a subject or problem that is understood by all involved.

A lot of time can be wasted if people in your group don't know the problem they are tryng to solve. Present the necessary background to the group.

3. Write all the ideas and objectives on a chalkboard or large sheet of paper where everyone can see.

If you are working alone, don't think you can get away without putting the random thoughts down. One of the secrets to brainstorming is having all the thoughts down on paper. Thoughts that seem crazy at first,

when combined with other seemingly crazy thoughts, yield extremely effective solutions sometimes. If you had not written down the wild ideas, you would not have been able to combine them to get the final superb creative solution. Use words, phrases, or pictures—anything that will rapidly capture the essence of the ideas as they flow from the individuals in the group. New and different relationships between the ideas expressed will cause additional ideas, but only if all the ideas can be seen together.

4. Concentrate on quantity not quality.

A great scientist once said "The way to get a good idea is to have lots of ideas." Produce as many ideas as possible; then you will have more from which to pick the best. It is easy, after a brainstorming session, to eliminate useless or ridiculous ideas. It is extremely difficult to "puff-up" a short list of ideas. Without *quantity*, you'll most likely not find the *quality* ideas either.

5. Keep it loose.

Nothing can stop good brainstorming more thoroughly than a leader with a Napoleon complex—a person who commands you to perform, who tries to *force* you to produce good ideas. Keep unnecessary structure out of it. The command "Get good ideas!" will do just the opposite by inhibiting their creation. What is needed is an open and free environment which gives an incentive for idea protection.

6. Hitchhike.

Let each person's thoughts build on another's ideas. Sometimes those off-beat and impractical ideas will trigger still other ideas that can be very useful. That ridiculous idea that you don't want to tell could prompt someone else to think of a smart one.

In brainstorming, don't narrow your vision—search all over in your experiences for 125 ideas that relate to the problem. You may find an idea in literature, yesterday's breakfast, or an insect's mating habits. Connect ideas that don't seem to belong together, and they may inspire the perfect solution.

The essence of getting good ideas is forming meaningful connections between knowledge and experiences in our lives. What would modern physics be like if Isaac Newton had not seen the connection between a falling apple and the bodies in the heavens? Where would modern medicine be without William Harvey making a connection between the functioning of a pump and the working of a human heart? How is a sunrise like hope, a cockroach like a tank, or a tree like a young boy? As Gyorgy Kepes, teacher and artist, once said, "The separation of our sensual, emotional and rational faculties into separate little slots is the prime reason for the formless nature of our environment and the lives we live."

7. No "no—no's."

Your goal is ideas, not judgments. By letting your mind run wild you can eliminate mental blocks to creative solutions. Don't judge what you or anyone else may think. If you have an idea, don't say to yourself, "I won't say it because they will think I'm stupid." And don't squelch someone else's dumb idea, either—it may stop him from participating, and you need his input. Judge the ideas generated in your brainstorming session *after,* not during the session.

8. Last is best.

The last half of a brainstorming session is often the best. It takes the first half to get all the usual responses and habitual solutions out of the way. When these are removed, what is left are new ideas and new ways of looking at the problem. Most idea sessions quit too soon, having generated nothing more than old mental clichés, nothing new.

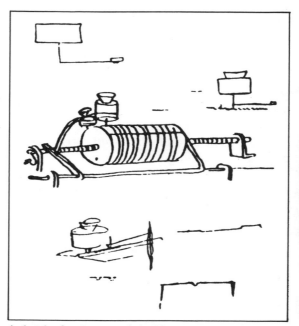

A sketch of a phonograph by Thomas A. Edison

Visualizing skills can increase the number of ideas you have and can improve their quality

Summary

We have been talking about how to get ideas. One thing that must be reemphasized is that ideas are only *thoughts*. And thoughts come and go in a flash. It's a major problem with creativity. You must find a way to retain the thoughts—the creative ideas. Don't let them just drift away never to be found again. Make the thoughts real; keep them. Get them down in black and white.

I do not know any truly creative person that could store truly creative new thoughts in his mind. Every great creative individual has put those thoughts down in some form or another. And you will find that most truly great innovative minds throughout history have relied on visual patterns to record their thoughts. If you go through the notes of Albert Einstein, Leonardo DaVinci, Issac Newton, Alexander Graham Bell, Albert Edison, or a hundred other truly great creative thinkers, you find their notes rich with visual images. They didn't just "write" their thoughts, they visually "sketched" their thoughts. If you want to be creative, you need to "capture" your thoughts. And a visual sketch of the thought can often be much more expressive than words used to describe the thought.

If you don't capture creative thoughts they will come and go just like the wind. That's just what this book is all about—capturing creative thoughts by rapidly sketching their essence. Great creative thinkers of the past might not be any more creative than you are. But they probably did one thing different than you are now doing—they put their thoughts down on paper so that we could see how creative they were. If you put your thoughts on paper you'll be amazed how much you already know, how creative you really are. Creative thoughts are nothing if they are not recorded. Make a resolve to begin today to sketch your thoughts. You will be delighted at the creative expanse your mind possesses.

We've covered many different things about getting good ideas. There are proven mental techniques that promote creative thinking. But you will notice that *every* creative process needs refinement. And, quickly writing or drawing that creative thought is important.

Creative thoughts don't jump out refined. The preceding paragraphs have explained how to get ideas started. This book tells you how to get the ideas finished. Get the ideas flowing, get them down on paper, then work them out. Ideas pop into the mind in embryo. They need rapid visualization—or some other form of graphic expression—to convert the fleeting thoughts into reality.

Exercises

Following are some visual exercises to improve creative potential. Let's get the ideas flowing and learn how to capture the thoughts before they float away never to be seen again.

A unique visual meaning for a common word

COMBAT

☐ *Pick any three of the words here and illustrate them.*

hot dog	tangle
chairman	usurp
warfare	fallacy
eastern	tissue
inhuman	tempestuous
flippant	hollow
headlong	safeguard
rubber band	winsome
defiance	underwear
dispute	
antidote	You choose
pigment	a fourth word
vengeance	to illustrate.

☐ *Force fit an item on the left with three items on the right to make a new product. (Force fit means to make them combine to form a new thing.)*

Fruits & vegetables	Things
grapes	apartment complex
apple	drawers
orange	jewelry
watermelon	computer terminal
corn on the cob	fountain
peas	telephone
tomatoes	protective helmet
rhubarb	wearing apparel
carrot	casegoods
bell pepper	light fixture
walnut	shoes
celery	air transportation
lettuce	water transportation
string bean	land transportation

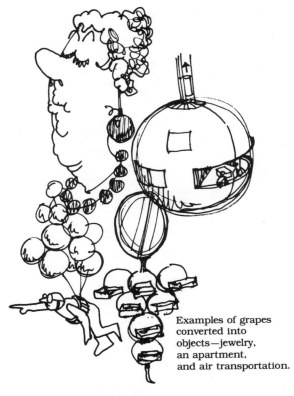

Examples of grapes converted into objects—jewelry, an apartment, and air transportation.

☐ *Use your imagination to create five new senses for humans. In addition to sight, taste, hearing, smelling, and touch, you now have a new sense. Illustrate that sense and explain what the sense is.*

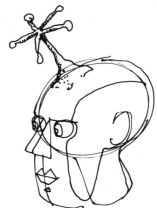

An example of the sense to always know the direction North

127

Some examples of things we may have in the year 2050

☐ We will have new technology in the year 2050. Illustrate ten of the new inventions that will be in use at that time.

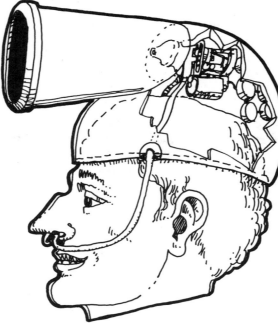

The Human Bloodhound in his Maxi-smell unit

☐ Create five inventions that will enhance one of your existing senses.

☐ Cut and paste items from magazines to create two new inventions. The inventions can be as realistic and useful as you want them to be.

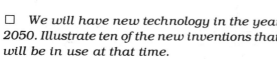

Throw-up Sheet

The doodles on the next page combine to form what I call a "throw-up sheet." This sheet is a catchall for the many ideas that emerged from my mind when given the assignment to create specific things. I find it fun to periodically make a new sheet about some wild idea just to keep my creative thinking powers sharpened.

☐ *Make a throw-up sheet that contains any one of the concepts listed below. Fill up the entire sheet with ideas about only the thing you choose from the list.*

better ways to carry clothes
better kinds of clothes
ways not to need any clothes
increased ways for getting information
directional lights
portable eating units
one-person transportation vehicles
one-person housing ideas
ways to grow food
things that expand and contract
    depending on the amount of light
things that use camouflage

☐ *Repeat the previous exercise, but do it with a group of people rather than alone.*

Note: a good place to get cheap paper for exercises like these is from printers that use web presses. The paper is on large rolls—the end of the roll is often not printed. These partial rolls can be purchased for a very reasonable price (many printers will give them to you).

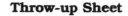

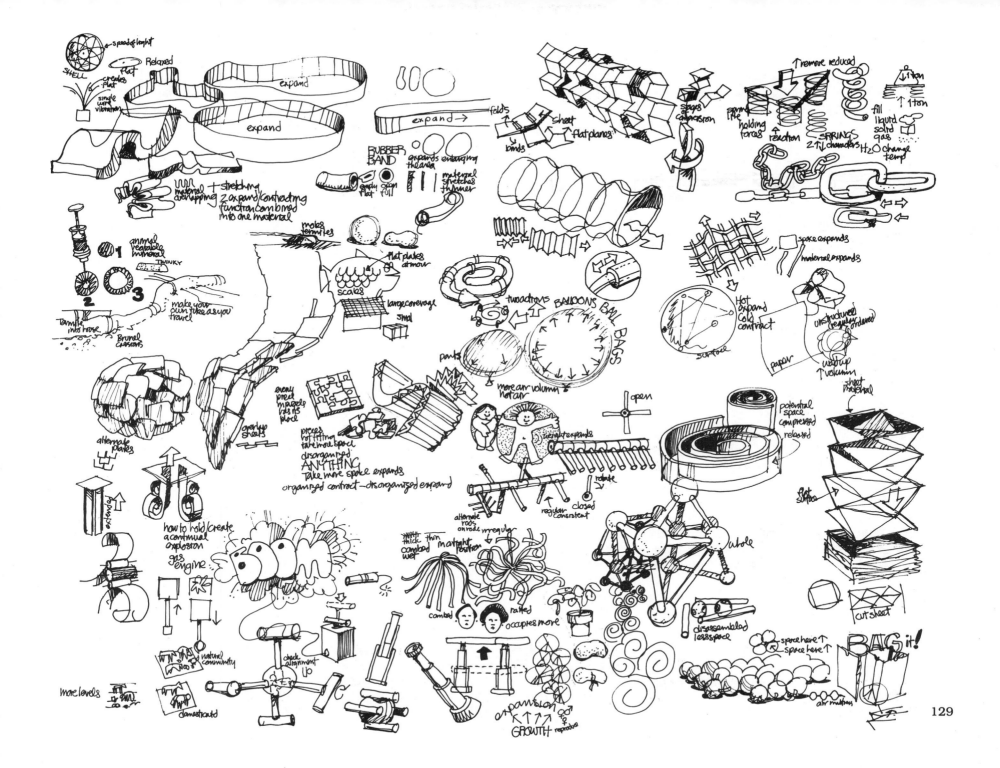

129

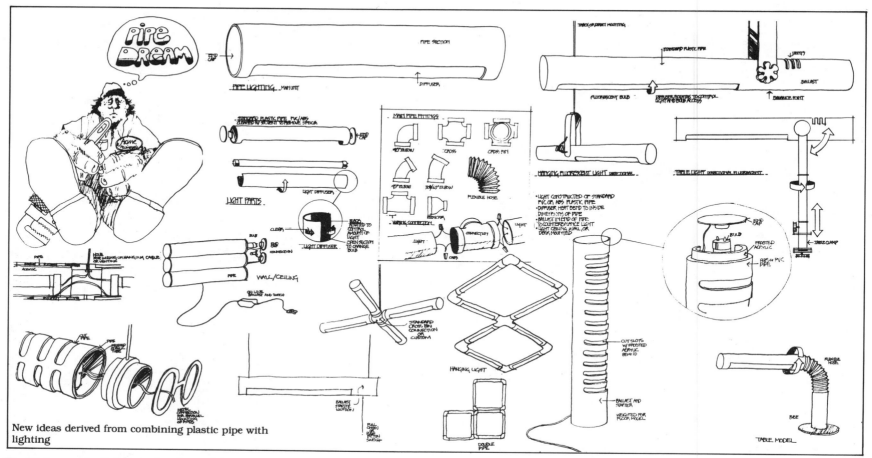

New ideas derived from combining plastic pipe with lighting

□ Take material or technology from one discipline and apply it elsewhere. Shown is a new form of lighting created by combining light fixtures with pipes. Listed are materials and applications: you combine any two you desire.

plastic pipe	lighting
50 gallon drums	moveable shelters
conduit	outdoor furniture
cement blocks	moveable exhibit
scaffolding	playground equipment
old tires	planter boxes
cable	exercise equipment
rocks	bedroom furniture

□ Design a musical instrument to be played by one of the following lifeforms.

octopus	bee
gerbil	ant
flea	giraffe
worm	bat
bird	alligator

□ Suppose that one of the lifeforms now living on this planet developed into an intelligent being. Years and years of evolution have transformed this lifeform into this new intelligent being. Draw one musical instrument that you think the new being would play.

An octopus's piano

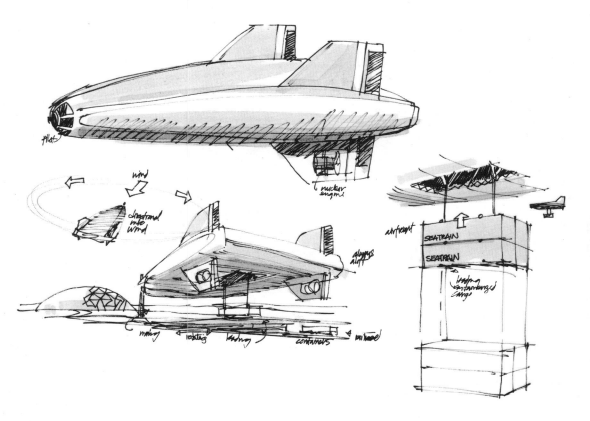

The national flag
A common medical practice
The winning float at the Grupla Winter Festival
Your choice

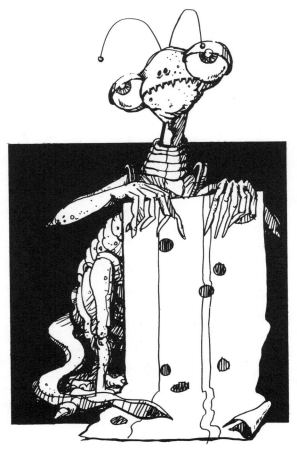

A Grupla holding the national flag

The winning float in the Grupla Winter Festival

☐ The future indicates we will have a great need for improving some of the following items. Pick two and illustrate how you will improve them for use in the future.

blimps and dirigibles
modular housing
emergency housing
maximum land utilization
new crop growing system
underwater vehicles
business offices
home recreation
clothing

☐ You have just had contact with the inhabitants of the planet Erpa Gruplas. You will want to illustrate for your friends what you have seen and learned about the inhabitants of this new planet. Illustrate at least three of the items listed.

One of the species of wildlife—a "Yozuca"
A favorite musical instrument—the "Cabushi"
A typical dwelling—a "Seemas-sassini"
Scenes from the latest box office hit—"Gone with the Mucker"
Clothing or jewelry worn on body phalanges
A favorite recreational pastime—"Ping"
A favorite meal—"Lingosplats"

131

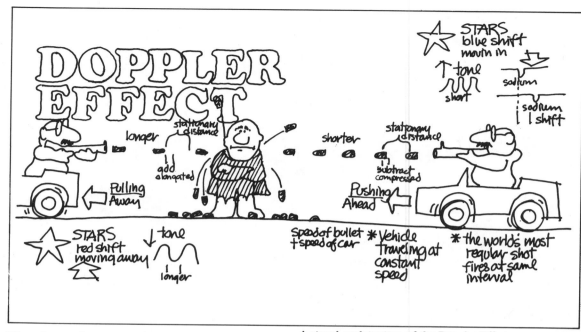

A visual explaination of the Doppler Effect

Learning with Visuals

Visuals can be a great help to learning, understanding and remembering. You are probably saying, sure, I have heard that before. A picture is worth a thousand words. It is easier to see and understand than to hear—but is it really true? Yes. Visuals can increase your ability to learn something. Let me relate a story about one student and how using visuals helped her. Then I will tell you in detail the process she used to improve her situation.

A True Story

Mary, a student at one of my classes, was doing well in art and design. She wasn't an outstanding student; she was an average student but she was working hard and doing well. One day, when she was very discouraged, she confided in me that she was not doing well in a psychology class. She told me that she just couldn't grasp the total concepts. She wasn't doing as well as she thought she should do. She was getting a C. She didn't want to get that kind of a grade—she wanted to get an A or a B. I told her about taking visual notes rather than verbal notes. I told her about structuring things with visual patterns, geometric shapes or doodle-type drawings, and that by using these visual notes that she should be able to understand and remember the subject more easily. After a thorough explanation she caught on to what I was talking about.

I did not get a chance to talk to her again about her psychology class until the end of the semester. One day she came into my office with a big smile on her face and proudly showed the A that she had earned. She claimed that the A was a result of visual notetaking. She said that drawing things out in visual patterns made it much easier for her to understand and then later to remember what she had learned in that psychology class.

This is only one example but, if space permitted, I could give many examples of how

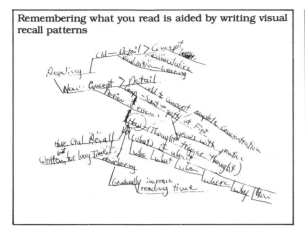

Remembering what you read is aided by writing visual recall patterns

it has worked for me and how it has worked for other people. For example, Evelyn Wood, nationally known teacher of speed reading, uses a visual note-taking concept to teach her students how to remember what they read in books. If you have ever been to an Evelyn Wood demonstration, you have seen students rapidly read many pages in a book and then recall in detail what they have read. Teaching them to read rapidly is only a part of Evelyn Wood's genius. I think the major help that Evelyn Wood gives these students is the ability to remember what they read. The way she does this is by teaching visual note-taking and recall to help the students remember things.

Visuals Aid Understanding

What is the strength of visuals to aid understanding? First of all, visuals help you see a whole picture, rather than just the small, individual parts. Visuals show a whole structure, at a glance, of what is going on. By seeing the whole structure, you can see the relationship of the parts. This whole structure and the relationship of the parts leads your mind to the details of the concept that you are trying to understand. By showing the whole and the relative parts at a glance, visuals make complex

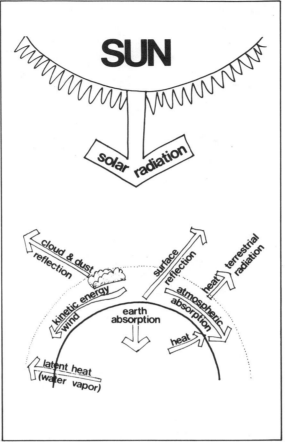

The weather on earth is affected by solar radiation   21

things easy to understand.

Let's discuss seeing the whole at one glance and how it works. Shown above is a visual of a very complex concept, weather conditions on earth resulting from heat gain and loss from solar/earth interaction. All that the example gives here is an overall view of how the system works, but by knowing that overall view, when you learn the details about the different things, then it becomes easy to put the details in perspective, to understand what the details relate to. You have seen the system's visual pattern. If I talk about the importance of

solar energy to life—how solar energy affects the weather and atmospheric conditions on earth—that makes sense because you can see how that happens. The details are easy to understand because you have seen the whole picture.

Another thing that visuals do is give structure to things. It is a human tendency *to seek order*. We want to have an orderly life. We want things *to make sense*. We want things to relate to something else. If something just seems to come out of nowhere or if we hear things that don't make sense, it is uncomfortable to us. Visual patterns are one way to help things to make sense. They form a picture of the relationship of parts. By relating things one to another we make sense out of things. So visual patterns feed our natural tendency to seek order; they help give order to the things that we learn.

Complex things are made easy to understand by tying the concept to a visual pattern. Structures give order to details. When we see the whole pattern of something, then it is easy to understand the parts. It is easy to understand the details if we can see the relationship of the parts. Visuals help complex things seem easy to understand.

A third way visual notes help is that the mind seeks strong mental images to recall. Visual notes are a strong mental image created for the mind to recall. This image makes it easier for the mind to picture what is happening and remember what is happening.

How To Take Visual Notes

Now that you have been shown that visual note-taking really can be an aid to understanding, let me explain how it is done. It is really very simple to take visual notes. You have only a couple of basic things to do. First of all, you need to develop some kind of structure. With a structure, you can tie the parts and the details

133

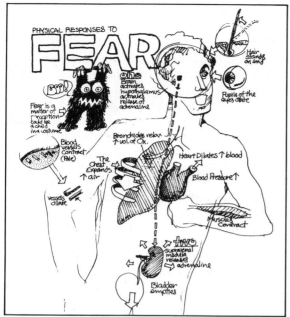

The physiological effects of fear

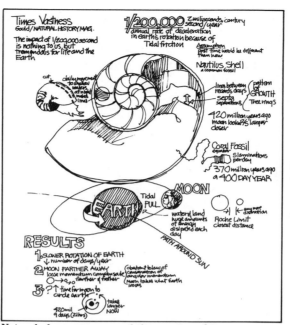

Natural phenomena record the passing of time

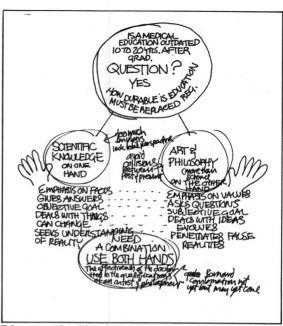

Education should include balanced learning

together so that everything will make sense; everything will be easily understood. How do you find that structure or develop that structure? Find a central theme of what you are talking about. Are you talking about cows or dogs or fear or government organization or exactly what?

Once you find that central theme, sort out the different elements that apply to it—the stories, the facts, the figures, the different details. You now put these elements around a central theme to form a relationship.

The example shown is the effect fear has on the human body. What is the reaction of the human body to fright? The central theme is *fear*—the physiological reactions the body has to fear. Now, what are the elements of that? As you look at the visual, you can readily see the different elements. Adrenaline enters the system, the hair stands on end, and so on. These are the basic physical and mental reactions

134

that occur when you are frightened. It's all very easy to see, easy to understand, and easy to remember. We just structure these elements around the body, where they happen. This is an example of how to take visual notes.

As you can see, we have drawn a fairly complex body here, but you could do the same thing with a very simple drawing, a very loose stick figure kind of drawing.

Other examples of visual note-taking are shown above. The illustration containing the snail is an explanation of the measurement of time using natural means as a clock to record the passing of time. The third visual showing the circles and the hands is a very simplified visual pattern about the need for education to include balanced learning in both scientific and artistic fields. Even though the information is written, the inclusion of the circles and hands makes a visual image for the mind to remember.

An easy method to use to develop a structure for visual note-taking is to ask obvious questions—Who? When? Where? What? Why? How? The questions themselves can be the central theme. The details or elements just answer the questions. These questions form a structure for understanding many different kinds of information.

Mark Twain—A Visual Note-taker

We talked earlier about the fact that visuals aid in remembering and recall. Let me relate a story that will illustrate the point.

Sometimes you have to speak—a sales conference, a convention, a testimonial dinner . . . whatever. You're scheduled to speak or you know you'll be called on.

So you worry. You organize your thoughts, sketch notes on a piece of paper, and you fret. You're normal.

You want the people to think the words just flow out; all the fresh anecdotes, the grasp of facts and detail, the humor. You want to do a good job, like the good speakers you've heard. But those good speakers don't talk from notes.

Are you going to pause and consult notes, thus admitting mere mortality? Or are you going to ad-lib, probably forgetting your best story and missing your most important point?

Mark Twain faced these problems once. He wasn't a speaker at first, but he became one of the most successful ones in American history. Twain worked out his system by trial and error and he didn't explain it until years later in an essay published after his death. The system was so good, he said, that twenty-five years after he'd given a speech, he could remember the whole thing by a single act of recall.

In his early days as a lecturer, Twain used a full page of notes to keep from getting mixed up. He'd write down the beginnings of key sentences to take him from one point to another and to prevent skipping. Typically, he'd write and memorize eleven key beginnings.

It didn't work. He'd remember the sentences but forget their order, so he'd have to stop, consult his notes, and spoil the spontaneity of the entire speech.

Then he decided not only to memorize the key sentences but also the first letter of each sentence. That didn't work either, not even when he cut the number of letters to ten and inked them on his fingernails.

"I kept track of the fingers for awhile," he wrote, "then I lost it, and after that I was never quite sure which finger I'd used last."

Twain says he considered licking off the inked letters as he went along, but people noticed he seemed more interested in his fingernails than in his subject. One or two listeners would come up afterwards and ask him what was wrong with his hands.

Then came the inspiration—the great

idea—that it's hard to visualize letters, words, sentences. *But pictures are easy to recall.* They grab you, and especially if you do them yourself.

"In two minutes I made six pictures with a pen," he reported, "and they did the work of 11 catch-sentences, and did it perfectly."

Twain was no artist, but he did them anyway. Having drawn the pictures, he found he could throw them away—he could recall their images at will (try it yourself).

Samples of his artwork indicate very crude drawings—maybe they're not art, but they did the job.

First a haystack with a wiggly line under it to represent a rattlesnake—to remind him to begin talking about ranch life in the West. Then there are slanting lines with what must be an umbrella under them and the Roman numeral II. That referred to a great wind that would strike Carson City every afternoon at 2 o'clock.

Next came a couple of jagged lines, lightning, obviously telling him it was time to move on to the subject of weather in San Francisco, where the point was that there wasn't any lightning, or thunder either, he noted.

From that day, Twain spoke without notes, and the system never failed him. He drew a picture for each section of his speech, all strung out in a row, then he'd look at them and destroy them. When he spoke, there was the row of images fresh and sharp in his mind. He'd make notes based on the remarks of a previous speaker—just insert another picture in your set of images.

Twain's method should be obvious to speakers who organize remarks around anecdotes. Draw in your own style whatever reminds you of the story. Often, the wilder the image, the easier it will be to remember. And it works as well for concepts as for anecdotes. Sales must go up—draw a vertically pointed arrow and a dollar sign. Research and

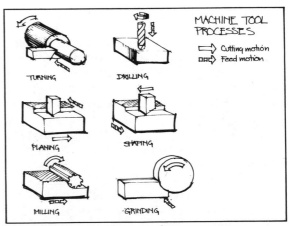

Visual explanation of basic machining processes

development—draw your own version of a scientist. Figures to remember—put them coming out of people's mouths, in pyramids, under a building . . . wherever. 22

Mark Twain was a writer. He could have written all the things down. But writing didn't work for him—it didn't help him remember as easily as visual patterns.

The same applies to nearly everybody. Visual patterns are a strong aid to remembering and recall. Why is that so? There are some simple reasons that visuals are such good helps to remembering.

Visuals Make a Unique Mental Image

First of all, visuals create a *unique mental image* that is easy to remember. If you look at words on a page you see a gray pattern; if you look at a visual picture, that visual picture is usually much different than any other visual picture you will see. This creates a mental image for the mind and that mental image is easy to remember—easy to recall.

Another thing is that visual pictures are a general overview. Visuals are a help because they take the mind from general to specific—

135

things are more easily remembered going from general to specific.

Another reason visuals help is that visuals *simplify* concepts. Remember the concept of the life support system? That drawing was very simplified. By understanding that simplified concept, then it is easy to understand the details.

A fourth reason visuals aid remembering and recall is the need for order that all individuals have. We want everything to make sense and have order. Visuals are an easy way to give order and sense to something, thus making it easy for us to memorize and recall what we see.

Make Your Own Visuals

Visuals that help you remember things work best if you make the visual yourself. It doesn't need to be fancy; it doesn't need to be complex; it doesn't need to be a great drawing; all it needs to be is a visual pattern. If you make the pattern, no matter what the pattern is, it is better than if you rely on someone else's pattern to help you recall something. Even if your pattern is much more sketchy and much more simple it will still work better than somebody else's complex pattern. Let me give an example of why that works and why you need to make your own patterns.

Have you ever heard of the term mnemonics? Mnemonics means using related sounds or concepts to aid memory to help the mind recall something. I had a friend that could not remember the name Alene Cook. So to help him he pictured in his mind an alligator that was leaning against a wall. This alligator had a cook's hat on because it was a cook. From that time on my friend had no trouble remembering the name Alene Cook. He pictured the alligator leaning against the wall with the cook's hat on. That visual picture that he created was a memory aid, an example of

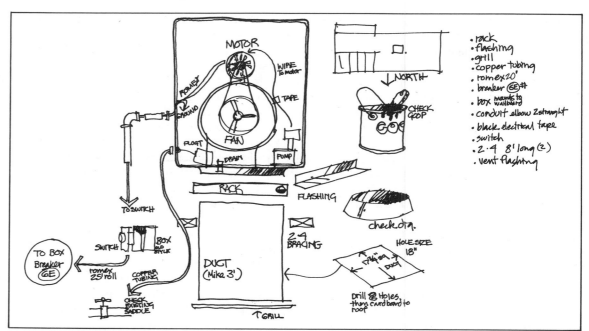

A drawing by a homeowner as he attempted to understand how to install a swamp cooler air conditioning unit

mnemonics. This same principle, as in mnemonics, of creating your own visual pattern is a good way to remember things.

The methods for creating visual memory patterns are the same as the ones you use for taking visual notes for understanding. You find a central theme, find all of the elements to that theme, then find a structure. No matter how strange the visual pattern—even as strange as an alligator leaning against the wall with a cook's hat—that structure will give relationship to the parts. Some examples of visual memory patterns are shown throughout this book. Geometric shapes—circles connected by lines, squares, lines coming out as the spokes of a wheel—are all visual patterns that can aid recall.

Rapid Viz Aids Learning and Recall

Using visuals can be a strong aid to understanding that often goes unused. Most people look at and remember visuals they encounter

in books. They notice a diagram in a book, which makes things easy to understand. But most people don't do their own drawing to create their own visuals to aid understanding. If you take visual notes, your ability to learn things will be increased greatly. Your ability to remember will also improve with your increased use of visuals.

We have discussed using visuals to aid understanding, to aid learning, to aid remembering. How does this relate to rapid visualization? Simply that if you are able to rapidly visualize a concept, you can easily take visual notes to aid understanding, to aid in learning, to aid in remembering. The principles that this book outlines about how to rapidly visualize things can be used to improve understanding and memory. Rapid viz helps you learn more easily and helps you remember what you learn.

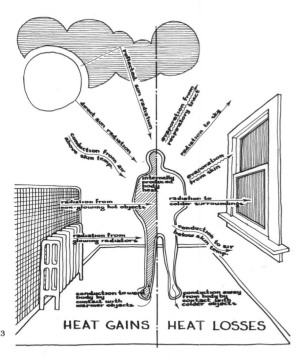

HEAT GAINS | HEAT LOSSES

☐ *Visually explain the following concepts. Some you will find to be complex—others you will find to be very simple. First determine the main points. Visually illustrate those points. Add necessary details later. (The example above explains the transfer of heat.)*

What is a characterization?
What is entropy?
What is euphemism?
What is structural stability?
What is harmony?
What is a network?
What is linear induction?
What is synergy?
What is an arms race?
What is a balanced budget?
What is injection molding?
What is platonic love?
What is deductive reasoning?
What is an ecosystem?
What is a heat pump?

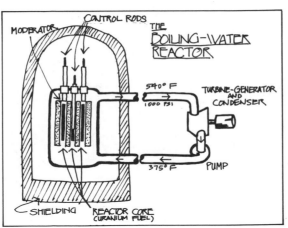

What is general system theory?
What is microeconomics?
What is transactional analysis?
What is offset printing?
What is a carbuncle?
What is a sterling engine?
What is meiosis?
What is the learning curve?
What is speciality advertising?
What are checks and balances?
What are soliloquies?
What is a manifold?
What is a legume?
Note: you know your visual explanation works when someone else can understand what you have illustrated.

☐ *Visually explain how to do any three of the following things:*
how to make bread
how to start a car
how to eat an apple
how to cut grass
how to dance the swing
how to evoke a response
how to follow a scent
how to cut your own hair
how to sell a wristwatch
how to make money
how to tie a shoelace
how to pick a nose
how to change a tire
how to install a lock
how to drill a well
how to write a poem
how to destroy a tank
how to play soccer

☐ *Watch an informational movie, TV show, or lecture. Be aware of the different visual explanations given to communicate the intended message. Take notes. Later refine your notes. Rethink the movie and compare your visual notes with those given. Compare your notes with another source (a resource book like an encyclopedia) that explains the same subject matter.*
Write what it was: _____
_____
_____
_____
_____
_____

☐ *Read two magazine articles. Take visual notes of what you read. Two or three weeks after reading the magazine article and making the visual notes look over the notes again. Reread the article. Determine how good your visual notes were for helping you remember what you read in the article.*
Magazine article one: _____
_____
_____

Magazine article two: _____
_____
_____
_____

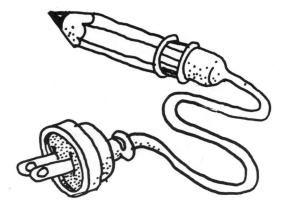

Exercises

The next few pages contain examples of exercises. As you do each, think about what you are doing. The exercises can serve as models to show you how to create similar exercises (either for personal study or to teach someone else) for future use.

□ *Learning to visualize can be achieved by causing your mind to see new views of objects. Draw a three-dimensional sectional view of the object described by the front, top, and side views of the objects shown. The section is as though you were to cut away a portion of the object.*

First Example

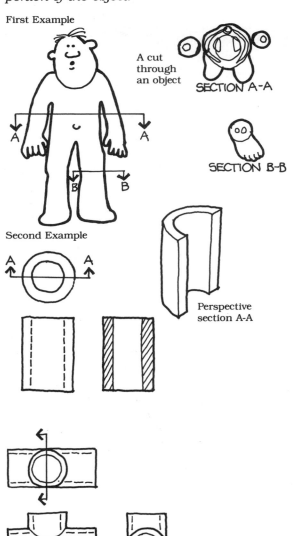

A cut through an object

SECTION A-A

SECTION B-B

Second Example

Perspective section A-A

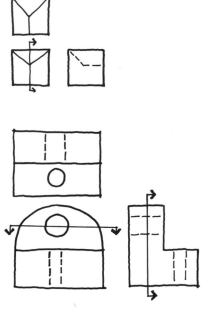

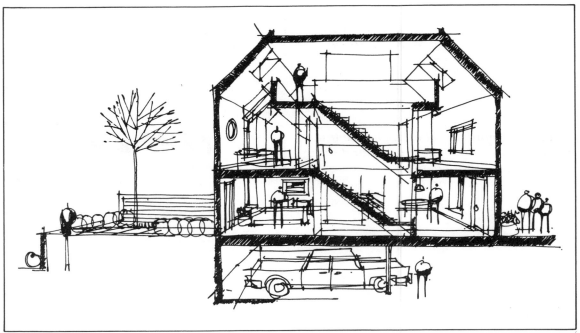

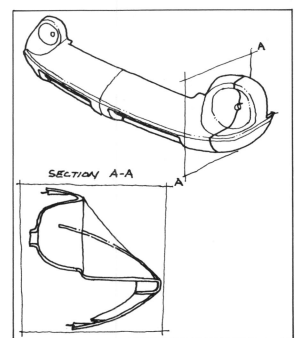

SECTION A-A

☐ Another good exercise for improving visualizing abilities is to see the internal workings of objects. Shown on this page are two kinds of techniques used to see internal parts. The van is shown as though the outer shell were transparent allowing you to see the internal parts. The hair dryer shows an exploded view of all the parts.

Find a small gadget or appliance that you can dismantle. Take it apart and draw the parts using either of the two techniques shown on this page—an exploded view or a transparent view.

A transparent view of a van

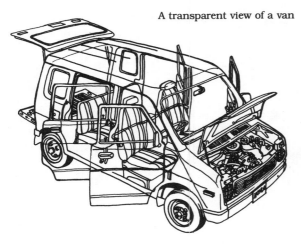

☐ Using the critical elements shown (light, switch, connections, batteries), design five different types of flashlights.

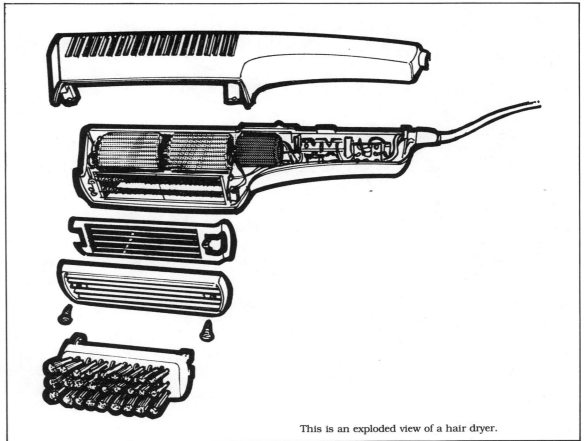

This is an exploded view of a hair dryer.

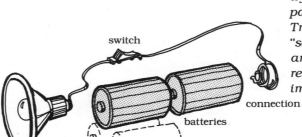

switch

light

batteries

connection

☐ This narrow street could be converted into a fabulous something. Lay a piece of tracing paper over the photograph (opposite page). Trace the structures. Now create a new "something" for the narrow street. It could be anything from a park to a rest area to a restaurant to whatever your mind can imagine.

□ Shown on this page are real and imagined views of playground equipment. Create a drawing of playground equipment that you would like to have built.

26

☐ *Transform this old house into a new structure. The new building need not, and probably should not, appear anything like the original house. Improve it in any way you can.*

This same technique of transforming something old into something new can be a source for numerous kinds of exercises.

144

□ *Grid sheets that analyze the different characteristics of a given situation can expand the visual mind. Study the one below to see how the grid pattern was used to analyze the problem.*

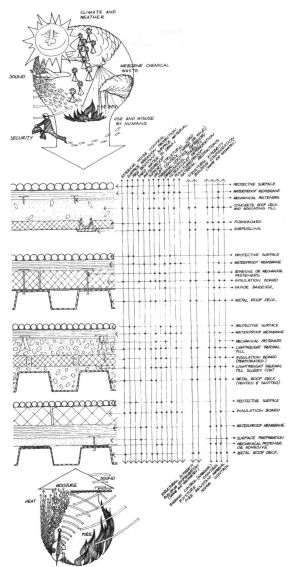

□ *Grid sheets are visual comparisons of two variables. The dots on the chart at left indicate where the items listed across the top correspond to the items listed down the right side.*

For you to get an idea of how grids work, determine two variables you can compare (how many men, women, and children walk along five different streets during different hours of the day, or anything else you desire) and express the information in the form of a grid. Grids are very simple to do. List one variable horizontally across the top or bottom and list the other variable vertically up one edge of the grid.

□ *Creating new objects from simple shapes expands visual powers. The circular restaurant was created by combining cylindrical shapes. Try a similar exercise by combining spherical or triangular shapes to create a new bank. Then, if you wish to go further, combine other basic shapes to create new wearing apparel, or new transportation equipment, or any other item you can imagine.*

☐ Can you think of any ways to improve this street? Make three drawings of ways this street could be improved or changed.

☐ The camper shown here could look completely different. Draw three different design ideas for changing the visual or functional aspects of this camper. Use tracing paper to help you quickly draw the basic parameters of the camper.

☐ One popular rapid visualization exercise is to create a flip visual. This is done by drawing step by step a cartoon show. Then staple all the visuals, one on top of the other, in order. Flip through the visuals as you would flip through the pages of a book. What you will see is a movie of the activity you have drawn.

Make your drawings on 3 x 5 cards. Put a thick rubber band around one end of the cards. Flip the other end of the cards to see the 'movie' of what you have drawn.

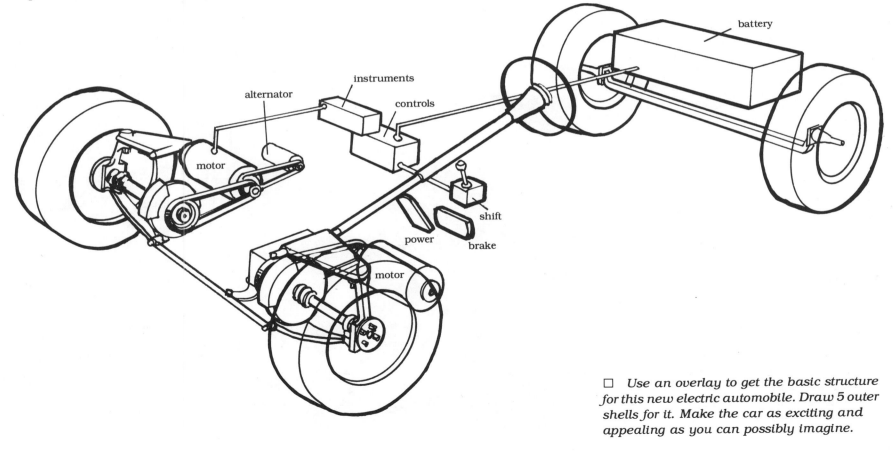

☐ Use an overlay to get the basic structure for this new electric automobile. Draw 5 outer shells for it. Make the car as exciting and appealing as you can possibly imagine.

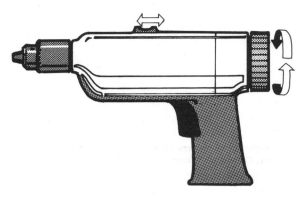

☐ Study the sequence illustrations shown. Duplicate the same kind of illustration but illustrate in seven sequences one of the following:

a ride in a car that you often take such as to work or to school
a walk through a school building
a walk through a park
a walk down a street near your home
a recent trip you took
a shopping trip to the grocery store

☐ Create a power hand appliance that does not need electricity as a power source. Your appliance can be a redesign of existing appliances in use today. Possible alternative power sources might include: wind, water, gravity, light, geo-thermal, fly wheels, etc.

27

☐ Imagine that someone named Fred Swartznikeldinger of Elko, Nevada has recently invented a "Matter Transporter." His device will transport matter from one location to another location instantaneously. Distance is no problem, for matter can be transported from one place to any other place in the universe as quickly as you can imagine it being there.

List 25 good results from Fred's new invention.

List 25 bad results from the invention.

Illustrate three of each of the good and bad results you have listed.

148

Special Consultant
Michael V. Lee

Visualizers
Scott Bevan
Stan Serr
Becky Miller
Carl Haynie
David Bartholomew

This book is designed to be folded, spindled, and mutilated.

Credits

If you have a new or different way to teach visualization, we would like to know about it. Or if you have any visual exercises that would be an improvement to the book, we would appreciate your suggestions. Please send your suggestions to the publisher.

1. U.S. Steel Corporation

2. An example by Dr. J. Richard Hayes found in the book *Towards A Theory of Instruction*, by Jerome S. Bruner, Harvard University Press

3. University of Utah Sports Department

4. Droodle Book Series, Roger Price, Price-Stern Publisher

5. Abstracta Systems, Inc.

6. Georgia Pacific

7. From the paper "Design Approaches to the Fibrous Glass Reinforced Polyester Bathroom as Related to Market Needs" by David D. Tompkins and Merritt W. Seymour, Owens Corning Fiberglass Corporation

8. Drawing by Carl Landow, Manhattan Community College, Caudill Rowlett Scott

9. John M. Johansen and Associates, by Ashoik M. Bhavnani, N.Y., N.Y.

10. Drawing by Howard F. Elkus, AIA Headquarters Building, The Architects Collaborative

11. Drawing by John M. Johansen, Leap Frog Housing, John M. Johansen & Associates

12. Reprinted from the January 1977 issue of Progressive Architecture, Copyright 1977, Reinhold Publishing Company, p. 73 (Richard Ridley and Associates)

13. *Introduction to Engineering Design and Graphics*, George C. Blakley and Ernest A. Chilton, The Macmillan Company

14. *Symbol Sourcebook*, Henry Dreyfuss, McGraw-Hill Publishing Co.

15. Drawing by Richard Dorman, Office Building, Dorman/Muirselle Associates

16. Drawing by Jim Hamilton, Seattle Center Hospital, Fred Bassetti & Company, Architects

17. Architects/Planners Alliance, Inc., Ralph F. Evans Architect, Developer/Owner Ralph F. Evans

18. Industrial Design Dept., Radio Corp. of America, Tucker P. Madawyck, Division Vice President

19. *The Metaphorical Way of Learning and Knowing*, W.J.J. Gordon, Porpoise Books

20. Paul Coker, Mad Magazine, E.C. Publications

21. Reprinted from the January 1977 issue of Progressive Architecture, Copyright 1977, Reinhold Publishing Company, p. 72 (Richard L. Crowther)

22. The Speechmaker's Quandry, Here's How Mark Twain Solved It, Educational Dealer, Jan/Feb 1977

23. Reprinted from the January 1977 issue of Progressive Architecture Copyright 1977, Reinhold Publishing Company, p. 68 (Burt, Hill & Associates)

24. Fiberglas/plastic design guide, prepared by Owens-Corning Fiberglas Technical Center, Market Development Laboratory Design Department under the direction of J.A. Keown, illustrations by D.A. Damico

25. Timberform, Inc.

26. Reprinted from the September 1978 issue of Progressive Architecture, Copyright 1978, Reinhold Publishing Company, p.123

27. *Architectural Illustration the Value Delineation Process*, Paul Stevenson Oles, AIA United States Pavilion Expo '67 (early scheme), R. Buckminster Fuller/S. Sadao

Through years of work and development, some people become knowledgable and skilled in particular subjects which have interested them. Often such people have compiled their information into a book, for the convenience and use of others. The following list includes some of the very best books prepared by authors with years of experience in drawing, visualization, teaching, and developing visualization experiences. Please take time to find and read them all—we are sure you'll find them to be very helpful.

Suggested Readings

Draw! A Visual Approach to Thinking, Learning, and Communicating, Hanks and Belliston, Crisp Publications, Inc.

Design Yourself!, Hanks and Belliston, Crisp Publications, Inc.

Drawings as a Means to Architecture, William Kirby Lockard, Van Nostrand Reinhold Co.

Design Drawing and *Design Drawing Experiences*, William Kirby Lockard, Pepper Publishing

Perspective—A New System for Designers, Jay Doblin, Whitney Library of Design

Graphic Problem-Solving for Architects and Builders, Paul Laseau, Cahners Books

Design with Nature, Ian L. McHarg, Doubleday Natural History Press

Pencil Broadsides, Theodore Kautzky, Van Nostrand Reinhold Publishing Company

Experiences in Visual Thinking, Robert H. McKim, Brooks/Cole Publishing Co.

The Natural Way to Draw, Kimon Nicolaides, Houghton Mifflin Co.

Perspective Drawing Handbook, Joseph D'Amelio, Tudor Publishing

Architectural Rendering, Albert O. Halse, F.W. Dodge Corp.

Seeing with the Mind's Eye, Mike and Nancy Samuels, Random House

Rendering with Pen and Ink, Robert W. Gill, Van Nostrand Reinhold

Visual Thinking, Rudolf Arnheim, University of California Press

Graphic Design for the Computer Age, Edward A. Hamilton, Van Nostrand Reinhold

Our World in Space, Robert McCall, Isaac Asimov, New York Graphic Society, Ltd.

Designers Dictionary, Bruce T. Barker, Tony Ken, The Upson Co.

The Pencil, Paul Calle, Watson-Guptill Publications

Language of Drawing, Edward Hill, Prentice-Hall

The Big Yellow Drawing Book, Dan O'Neill, Hugh O'Neill and Associates

Innovations, United States Steel Corporation

Archigram, Peter Cook, Praeger Publishing

Drawing the Head and Figure and *How to Draw Animals*, Jack Hamm, Grosset & Dunlop

Architectural Delineation, Ernest Burden, McGraw-Hill

Drawings by American Architects, Alfred M. Kemper, John Wiley & Sons

Architectural Illustration—The Value Delineation Process, Paul Stevenson Oles, Architectural Press.

The new *Drawing on the Right Side of Your Brain* (now in bookstores)